"Lonnie Joseph Nichols has presented us with a text that is as multifaceted and holistic as his philosophy. The affirmations and meditations will benefit students of every meditative discipline. The understanding he brings to the energetic nature of healing should be incorporated in medical, chiropractic, acupuncture, and massage schools throughout the land. The techniques and concepts Mr. Nichols espouses work and are repeatable; they place the power of healing in the hands of the patient where such power belongs."

—Dr. Robert Kienitz, D.Ac., M.Sc.O.M.
Director of the Stone Pointe Institute of Oriental Medicine
Mesa, Arizona
Dean of Faculty and Curriculum,
Phoenix Institute of Herbal Medicine and Acupuncture
Scottsdale, Arizona

"I have learned many things from my friend and mentor, Lonnie Nichols. Lonnie started out as my patient and has become my teacher. In *The Soul as Healer*, he gives you [the reader] gems of his own inner wisdom and helps you recognize the healer within you."

—Dr. David Vicena, D.C.
Host of the Talk Show, *Natural Healing Arts*
Mesa, Arizona

About the Author

L. Joseph Nichols draws on a multifaceted background and experience to teach and apply his healing techniques and knowledge in energy work. Over the past twenty years he has led various spiritual, meditation, and metaphysical classes and workshops, healing groups, and he works closely with individual clients to release old, limiting patterns. He is the author of *God, the Universe, and Self* (DeVorss & Co., 1982), as well as a number of health-related newsletters.

He is currently a program manager with a worldwide telephone corporation, where he manages ground systems for Southeast Asian satellite communications. He is also a staff member at Stone Point Institute Acupuncture Center in Chandler, Arizona.

To Write to the Author

If you wish to contact the author or would like more information about this book, please write to the author in care of Llewellyn Worldwide and we will forward your request. Both the author and publisher appreciate hearing from you and learning of your enjoyment of this book and how it has helped you. Llewellyn Worldwide cannot guarantee that every letter written to the author can be answered, but all will be forwarded. Please write to:

L. Joseph Nichols
℅ Llewellyn Worldwide
P.O. Box 64383, Dept. K487-1
St. Paul, MN 55164-0383, U.S.A.
Please enclose a self-addressed stamped envelope for reply,
or $1.00 to cover costs. If outside U.S.A., enclose
international postal reply coupon.

THE
SOUL
AS
HEALER

Lessons in Affirmation, Visualization, and Inner Power

L. JOSEPH NICHOLS

2000
Llewellyn Publications
St. Paul, Minnesota 55164-0383, U.S.A.

FIRST EDITION
First Printing, 2000

Book design and editing by Connie Hill
Cover images from Pixar and Aztech New Media Corp.
Cover design by William Merlin Cannon

Library of Congress Cataloging-in-Publication Data
Nichols, L. Joseph, 1948–
    The soul as healer : lessons in affirmation, visualization, and inner
power / L. Joseph Nichols — 1st ed.
       p.   cm.
    Includes bibliographical references.
    ISBN 1-56718-487-1
    1. Mental healing. I. Title.
RZ400.N46 2000
615.8'52—dc21   00-027492

Llewellyn Worldwide does not participate in, endorse, or have any authority or
responsibility concerning private business transactions between our authors and the
public.
   All mail addressed to the author is forwarded but the publisher cannot, unless specifically instructed by the author, give out an address or phone number.

The methods and treatments in this book are not meant to replace professional medical care. Although all of these techniques have proven successful, the author and the
publisher take no position on their effectiveness.

Llewellyn Publications
A Division of Llewellyn Worldwide, Ltd.
P. O. Box 64383, Dept. K487-1
St. Paul, MN55164-0383, U.S.A.
www.llewellyn.com

Printed in the United States of America on recycled paper

Dedicated to my three daughters:
Faith Victoria, Teresa Angela, and Anitra Lorraine

Contents

Acknowledgments

I would like to thank my first teacher, and spiritual companion, Sandra Faye, for her endless support, love, and wisdom. Her example of unconditional love gave me the confidence and spiritual base to pursue my spiritual path over twenty-five years ago. That momentum continues throughout the following text. I thank Dr. Trevor Creed for his selfless teaching and endless energy in introducing the powerful techniques of Chironic Healing to the United States, and around the world. I would also like to thank Jan Trenorden Thomas for her contributions in the development of the modality of these same techniques, as well as Andrew Creed for his graphic designs, artwork, and his strong, continued support of the Chironic Healing community.

Equally important to me have been the many Souls who have requested my assistance in their healing process, since they have been my best teachers of all. Without them, this book would not have been possible.

Introduction

The concept of healing remains foreign to many of us, even though the field of holistic health has become very popular in recent years. Healing should not be an uncommon term in our vocabulary, however. Numerous activities and processes of healing are occurring within all of us, all of the time. Our physical bodies are continually repairing themselves at the cellular level, while our emotional bodies are experiencing feelings that trigger our minds to consciously process the discord and discomfort we sense in our feeling world. Indeed, *healing is an integral process of life*, not merely a concept.

It is natural for most of us to consider healing as an activity that we seek when we do not feel well, yet the innate healing process is continually at work at all levels of our being. A general view of the field of healing includes all types of practitioners: medical doctors, massage therapists, psychologists, acupuncturists, counselors, Reiki healers, etc. And, yes, your hair stylist may be your best therapist, providing you the emotional healing you need on Saturday mornings to jump-start your weekend.

Clearly, healing is a combination of integrated processes transiting each and every level of our being, reflecting the magic of life itself.

Healing is not just a rebuilding of the body's cells, or the process of emotional healing through an open discussion with your therapist. Healing can occur while you are helping an elderly person cross the street, sending a kind card to your mother, or providing encouragement to a distraught friend. *Healing has its foundation in the energy of love,* and therefore is unlimited in the ways it may manifest in your life.

We may choose to be specific in our healing techniques, and we may choose specific individuals to help us in times of need, but the real healing of another human being is not limited to any technique or practitioner. *Healing another or ourselves consciously is only limited by our own mind and, more importantly, by the love in our heart.* The faith and openness of the patient is an integral factor as well, as we will explore in the following pages. Some of my most blissful personal experiences in this area have occurred in the back rooms of retail stores, the hallways of corporate offices, or sitting at the local pub lending an ear to a friend. Healing is as available to us as the air we breathe, and the energy for it is both unlimited and free. *To heal is to make whole, and making ourselves whole embraces the very core and reason for our existence—the very essence of life on Earth. Healing accelerates our growth.*

Clearly, on a regular basis new techniques, modalities, and concepts are emerging that treat and sometimes even cure those ailments once considered incurable. Modern science and technology have helped improve exponentially the quality of life on Earth for us humans, and our lifespan is ever increasing, while the fear of many diseases is diminishing in an equally incremental fashion.

But another process, that of self-healing, is also emerging in our culture. The elements of this process are as varied as the individual, but include such concepts as the effects on the body of the emotions and of thought, sending specific thoughts to a body part, meditation, relaxation, biofeedback, past-life karma, etc. I have found personally that there is indeed great power in mental healing and visualization. Moreover, thousands of cases have been documented that concur with this belief.

Yet with all of these proven cases, only a small percentage of people seek to heal themselves, to search out the underlying potential cause of a chronic problem. Why? It is much easier to go to someone else and pay them to heal you. It is much easier to treat repeatedly a symptom that may have at its root an emotional scar from the past, than to evaluate your underlying emotional pattern and resolve the issue once and for all. It takes a lot of courage, strength, and honesty to become fully responsibly for one's personal health. We have taken the easy way out for quite some time.

The issue is not completely what is easy or what is not; the issue is ownership of our health, ownership of our life. When one takes ownership, the ability to heal the self is simply a by-product of his or her life pattern. As an intelligent culture, we owe it to ourselves to not only seek this ownership, but to explore the more subtle powers of the mind. It has been our nature to explore the Earth and the stars around us, to venture "out there," yet our Western tendencies do not encourage an introspective search of our inner nature, our inner potentials. In this arena, I must agree with the great mathematician that we utilize only 10 percent of our brain. This tendency to seek "out there" is perhaps the greatest shortcoming of our Western culture.

Returning to my own personal experience(s), which I will elaborate upon in Chapter III, there is one particular experience in self-healing that is indeed a primary force, and added to my motivation to write this book. It proved, beyond all doubt, the power of the mind and of the Spirit. I have been blessed to experience just a tiny fragment, a miniscule portion, of the powers within me. I will share that experience with you later.

Nearly all of the writing I have done as an adult has been either of a metaphysical or inspirational nature. That general tone carries over into this work as well. It is true in the healing process, as in all aspects of life, that certain laws are at work, and I have delineated most of these laws and principles where appropriate throughout the text.

When I started this book, my intentions were to bring to print all of the techniques I had discovered and used that I knew worked—some were quite practical, while others were much more etheric and abstract. I had found that many teachings were not working for me, and at the same time I was discovering methods that were not taught anywhere but that did indeed work quite well. I also wanted to provide a general outline, a definition of healing, and, to some extent, present a discussion on the structure of our being in terms of the *energetic configuration*. This discussion includes some of the energetics of the world around us as well.

As I proceeded with the text I was able to bring forth, much to my surprise, some of the more subtle aspects of healing. These levels are of course where the real power of personal healing lies—in the subtle realms of the mind, the emotional nature, and in the intricate energy field that surrounds all of us. The most astounding aspect in this process was the fact that I was bringing forth many experiences that I had not previously realized consciously. It was only through the written word, drawing upon those many quiet moments of thought, that I was able to capture those experiences and processes that were at work in my life as a healer. Only through writing this book was I able to assimilate many of these processes consciously. In that regard the following pages serve me very well.

Much of this *energy work* transpires in an unconscious manner because of the intimate nature of one-on-one healing and the simple fact that our conscious mind can only process and retain so much information at once. The biggest reason many of these experiences remained somewhat hidden within my consciousness was because when one is in the *healing consciousness*, or healing energy, the mind shifts out of the conscious level. When we attune to a client and allow our High Self to work, we are not in a conscious state, as we usually know it. Our state or level of awareness becomes intuitive and often superconscious. We all have this ability, these subtle and powerful levels of energy available to us—believe it!

We will begin by laying the groundwork for healing on the premise that *all is energy,* followed by some vantage points on personal, as well as cosmic energy. These first two chapters are both relatively abstract when viewing the universe as energy in motion, yet very practical to the healer when working in another's field. The focal point of the text in terms of essential healing techniques and principles lies in Chapter III, "Principles in Self-Healing." The processes and techniques outlined in this chapter apply to all areas of healing, not just healing the self. I describe and employ such techniques as visualization, affirmation, and meditation, which have proven to be successful for many. My experience has shown me that those who have learned about themselves and have begun to heal themselves can apply those principles in healing others quite easily. *To truly understand another's inner condition, we must first understand ourselves.*

Finally, I touch on the principles in healing others, truly the extension of healing ourselves. There are some obvious differences, but surprisingly there are more similarities than you might imagine. Chapter V outlines an introductory lesson in Chironic Healing techniques that reestablishs the perfect pattern in the human aura, allowing the body to heal itself. These teachings are relatively new, originating in Australia just a few years ago.

It is my hope that the following pages will provide a number of elements for the reader. It is at once a statement of proven techniques and principles in healing energy, while at the same time a partial foundation for the *Laws of Life*, as I understand them. These laws and principles obviously apply to all of us— not just to those in the health care field. A primary intention of mine is to provide inspiration and workable information in the field of healing for those at all stages of development. For the beginner, there are practical tools and principles on which to build your art, and for those of you who are accomplished healers, the following pages may open some new doors that will supplement your work. It is a guideline and a text—one that I hope will serve as a reference manual and an inspiration to anyone interested in helping others as well as themselves. Additionally, it is a statement and reflection of my current status as a healer—a status that is constantly growing and expanding!

Never forget the power of common sense and practicality when confronted with serious health issues. Although all of the methods and techniques in the following pages will potentially work, they do so over time. They do not replace practical medical attention when needed, nor do they apply in many emergency situations. The traditional medical approach has saved countless lives and restored just as many to good health. We owe the medical profession great respect for this, and we owe ourselves an equal respect when it comes to the condition of our body. Know when to meditate and use your herbs—and know when to get to a doctor!

As with all information of a metaphysical and spiritual nature, you must find those elements that work for you. Trust your intuition. Learn to experiment with your hands, your heart, and your mind. Open up to the vast energy of healing available to you! And, learn to trust your Soul in its journey toward perfection!

I AM LOVE

I Love and accept myself as I am. All my imperfections are
washed away with this all-consuming Love. The Father of All
Loves His creation unconditionally . . . and I am one with
this Love.

I send Love to all my body, and I know it is well. I send Love to
my feelings, and I know they are healed. I am Love Manifest.
I forgive myself for not always knowing.
I forgive myself for not always feeling Love.
I Love myself for all my imperfections.
I Love myself totally in this moment.

When I doubt, I Love myself for doubting.
When I feel lack, I Love myself for this feeling, for it is only
Love that will evaporate the doubt and quench my heart's
thirst.
I Love myself for misunderstanding. My new Love will bring
wisdom to my heart.
I Love and Forgive myself for hurting others, for my lack of
Love was my only error.
I forgive myself for my emptiness, and I march forward with
my Army of Love to heal those around me with Forgiveness.
My new Love glistens in my heart as the dew on the shimmer-
ing, green meadow. It sings in my Soul like a songbird's symphony in the springtime, and it cleanses my Being as a
waterfall's mist douses the crisp evening air.

Yes, I Am Love, relentlessly pursuing your heart. You have
looked here and there for me, yet I have waited patiently to
fulfill the real dreams and desires of your eternal nature.

Many times when you have doubted, I awaited as you fought your self-created battles. And now the battlefield is clear, and you have conquered the enemy within by allowing me to enter through your heart as your commander-in-chief.

Many times you have believed yourself to be separate from Love. Love is what you are and what you have always been.

Loving yourself is truly all that there is . . . since All is Love, I AM LOVE.

I
Energy and Healing

There are many forms and modalities of healing. In all cultures of our known history, various forms and methods of healing have been used to help our human condition. No matter what form is used, though, or what malady is being attended, *love* must be the foundation. All of the knowledge in the universe cannot completely heal without the fuel of love to direct the innate healing energies from the heart and from the Soul.

The following pages contain much philosophy and a fair amount of intellectual premise that should help you reach an understanding and focus when working with the healing process, but we must never overlook the real source of all healing: *love—love of others and love of self.*

To understand how any form of healing works, we must first take a look at the nature of self and what it is that we are healing. This "what" turns out to be energy, or energy fields that require repair and realignment. First we'll look at some general perspectives of energy, and then we'll take a closer look at our personal energy fields.

I recall early in my senior year of college asking one of my professors, "Just exactly what is energy?" Needless to say I did not receive a response that satisfied me, only answers like: "Well, it performs work," or, "It's what makes heat and light," or, "It takes energy to climb stairs." These are all *reflections* and *results* of energy, but are not true definitions of energy. My inquisitive mind wasn't satisfied, and I now believe that my drive for total understanding from a physical level was the fuel that propelled me into the metaphysical arena. The metaphysical laws began satisfying my thirst for the deeper knowledge and understanding of the laws at work in our universe.

We sense energy all of the time—in the sunshine, in the processes of our physical body, in the constant activity around us in our daily lives. We intuitively know that it is the source of all that we know of as life, and it appears to be that all-powerful *something* that indeed gives us life and sustains us.

Energy Is Life

Our personal lives are full of energy—physical energy, commencing with the chemical energy and processes at the cellular level; emotional energy, the force that fuels our greatest ambitions and defines our basic personality composition; and mental energy, which gives us direction, clarity, and eventual understanding and integration in the world in which we live. The intertwining and overlaying of these three building blocks of our personality is what makes us so unique. Add to this our personal quota of spiritual energy and we become quite an intricate energy field.

However, the complexities of our individual personalities and the energies at work in our lives represent only a portion of the total energies available to us and are within reach of our consciousness. Vast, multidimensional energies exist within and around us at all times, though we are usually not aware of them. One of the great challenges before us at this stage in our evolution is to tap into this free energy and use it in our spiritual as well as our daily lives.

Healing involves energy, whether we're working with our hands, our minds, or our hearts. Healing by definition implies an imperfect condition, and imperfection to the healer implies an energy block of some type. To correct these blocks, to remove them, or to simply move the energy around, we must understand these basic building blocks of energy that make us what we are. We'll look at the details of our identity as it relates to healing more closely in Chapter II, but first let's examine the essence behind the *persona*.

Soul Energy

As personalities we possess a physical body, emotional body, and a mental body. (By "body," I mean a specific range, or frequency of energies.) We are discovering very rapidly that these three bodies or energy fields cannot be isolated, or totally separated—they are interwoven as our persona—developed over time. This is the real fabric of our personality—the energies of *mind, body,* and *emotion.* The products of these are *thought, the physical body,* and *feeling,* respectively.

Additionally, there is a spark of energy behind this three-fold matrix. This spark, or essence, which drives or utilizes our personality, is the Soul, or High Self. As we grow and learn to express more completely and clearly, we become a four-fold creature—our Soul uses the vehicles of body, mind, and emotion to express itself. This is what spiritual growth is all about—the ability to manifest our Soul, and our Divine purpose. Stated another way: *The Soul is manifesting through the vehicles of mind, body, and emotion. The more clearly it manifests its purpose through these vehicles, the more evolved an individual becomes in our world.*

Our four-fold nature, the combination of the personality and the soul, can be compared to the model of the physical atom of the physicist. As in the atom, there is a nucleus—let's call it a "Soul"—with three primary electrons rotating and spinning about it—let's call these the physical, mental, and emotional bodies.

The early image and understanding that scientists had of an electron was that it circled a nucleus in a precise, symmetrical pattern. This model no longer applies. It has now been determined that the electrons move and spin in similar orbits, but they are located in probability patterns and locations. In modern physics the electron's path around the nucleus is viewed essentially as this probability pattern, or field. This analogy is more accurate, since what we are and how we behave are truly probabilities—not certainties! From the physicist's viewpoint, each sub-atomic particle can be further subdivided many times. At each step of this process, scientists are realizing that the atom is not really made of matter, but of energy. In essence, there is nothing truly solid in our world! All is energy!

Similarly, our physical, emotional, and mental bodies are dynamic, fluctuating, and are expanding toward the probabilities and potentials that our soul has set into motion prior to birth. And, as in the atom, these bodies can be subdivided into many parts, all of which can be viewed as composites of energy. In summary, our existence, our future, and our personality are predicated on probabilities, not science.

The Soul's purpose may be to incarnate primarily for growth, for stability, for the resolution of past relationships, or it may be as grandiose as becoming a great leader of a country, an inventor, or a dynamic speaker. A key ingredient to personal health is to be in alignment with this Soul purpose. We are born with certain, agreed-to lessons and general purposes to complete in our lifetime. Within that agreement are lesser, more numerous tasks and experiences that we want to also complete.

This understanding helps the healer in discerning some of the probable causes of a patient's problems, as well as the possible lessons the person must learn. Obviously we cannot, nor should we, know all of the details of the individual, but with experience and intuition, the healer can be guided through reading the body and sensing the emanating energies that are important for healing.

Many times we don't realize when we are healthy or feel great, simply because it is the natural state of being. At these times we are usually aligned with our soul's purpose. We feel alive and happy! We do, however, recognize when we're not feeling good, or our energy is low—these periods are always very obvious!

Our major lessons, as we are learning them, tend to be reflected in the health of our physical body. Once the lesson is completely learned, the reflection, or ailment, greatly improves or vanishes. Behind all physical ailments there are incorrect thought patterns, discordant feelings, or a major lesson to be learned. Most illness reflects some combination of these three.

That's not to say we are necessarily doing anything wrong, only that we're usually clearing out and moving forward in our consciousness, unless of course it is a chronic, repetitive condition. When situations tend to repeat themselves it is usually a signal that we haven't learned our lesson. Our soul will keep bringing back the same old issues until we do learn our lesson(s).

One basic principle in all healing is that true healing must come from within the individual Soul level. Sure there are many good facilitators for healing, all appropriate and necessary at times in our growth, but only the individual Soul, the spark within, can unleash the healing energies required to permeate the many layers and levels of our being and usher in the healing power.

The Soul is always the primary healer.

◆

Soul is our connection to Source. Our individual Soul leads us to the experiences we require for our best and highest growth in our lives. This Soul is our personal "Christ Awareness," representing the Christ principles within all of us.

Just what is the "Soul"?

There are many definitions and references to "Soul" in the philosophies and religions of the world. For the purposes of healing and understanding individual energies, the Soul can be generally viewed as the *real self*, or the underlying *essence* of being that is pure, all-knowing, and has retained the experiences of all previous lifetimes.

The Soul is our personal connection with God, or Source. It acts as a type of mediator between our unfolding personality and Source. Other names are "High Self," "Christ Self," "Essence," etc. In the healing process, we must have a basic belief in this central, governing aspect (Soul) in order to understand the underlying energy, which helps us facilitate the healing process.

From an energy standpoint, there are two general causes for disease and imperfection in our physical dimension:

♦ Our Soul creates a malady, a handicap of sorts, in order for us to learn a specific lesson, or lessons, or,

♦ There is simply a blockage, lack, or overactivity of energy in a certain area of the body. Generally, this second scenario is *the result of errant thinking, fueled by discordant feelings from the emotional body.* Over time, the energies of wrong thought and emotions of discord are always reflected in the physical body. These two general causes tend to interplay with each other. Let's look at them a little more closely.

Lessons for the Soul

We are all born in this world with a preexisting agreement at the soul level to accomplish a certain degree of growth or mastership in this dimension of life. As a sort of corollary to this process, many individuals are born with karmic handicaps; i.e., a cause-and-effect condition, in which they themselves manifested as a result of an affliction to someone else. That's not to say that all handicaps are personal karmic debt. They may be, or they may be chosen to learn a new lesson. The healer does not judge this, but only asks at the soul level that healing be appropriate.

Remember that effective healing will only take place when the individual Soul allows it. An example of this might be an individual who agrees to learn patience in his or her life. Perhaps one way to do this is to agree to not have the use of their legs. Perhaps this individual spent many lifetimes as a bossy, irritable type, showing no patience with those of lesser abilities or talents. The Soul realizes that for the individual to be complete in their growth, he or she must now learn patience. Spending a lifetime as an immobile person, depending somewhat on others may help consummate the Soul's growth in learning these qualities of patience with self and gratitude for others.

The possibilities are infinite, but the point is that the Soul has made the agreement in order to learn a lesson. This lesson is usually in conjunction with balancing their cause and effect balance sheet carried over from life to life.

Unless a lesson is learned completely, and the purpose of the ailment has been accomplished, no amount of healing of any type will provide permanent relief. There may be partial or temporary relief, and in the process the patient may be awakened to the real cause of the problem.

> *Only the Soul can decide when the lessons are learned. The manifestation of perfection and health on all levels is totally dependent on this. It is the law.*

This understanding is critical for all health practitioners to remember in treating their patients. That's not to say that there shouldn't always be a positive effort placed on all healing and treatment with the intention of alleviating suffering! When our healing intention has its foundation in love, we can often awaken patients to their own Soul, even if there is no immediate effect on the physical level; *this awakening to the Soul is indeed the greatest service one can provide another being.*

Even when the Soul is not giving complete permission for healing to take place, *the individual's consciousness is still being accelerated and uplifted.* One of the beauties of seeking healing and sorting out all possible causes of an illness or ailment is that the process itself is extremely healing and Soul expanding. Most of us know many people who, after seeking standard medical help for an affliction, have turned to holistic methods and found not only much relief, but they expanded and enlightened themselves spiritually in the process. More and more people are looking to understand the cause of the problem, and not simply to treat the symptom.

It may be said that we come into our world at present to *experience and expand in consciousness*—to grow, to learn, to experience material life, to mend relationships, etc. If this is true, then the general field of healing, that of making whole again, is one of the most rapid paths. This process begs us to re-evaluate, process, and eventually transmute each and every particle in the fabric of our being.

Our connection with our Soul, or High Self, is not only critical to our well-being, but is exactly the process that many of the Eastern religions and philosophies have been teaching for thousands of years. To a great extent, our Western culture has lost the connection with Source and with this Soul that we've been talking about. We've heard this before, but what does this mean?

The process of healing accelerates the consciousness of both the one being healed and the healer. Both are on parallel paths—the expansion of consciousness.

Obviously we can only postulate, or at best intuit, such a connection, until we are reconnected (then we'll know, right?). In other words, we cannot fully understand and comprehend a consciousness vaster than ours with our limited human tools. Our tools need to be refined. In a way, our dilemma is not unlike the early scientists who could not see the tiny particles of matter without the proper microscope.

To understand this idea of *lost soul*, let's journey for a moment to the following possible scenario. As healers it will provide us an overview of the predicament or situation in which many of us currently find ourselves:

> At the beginning of time there was God, or Source—an all-pervasive, all-knowing "Love/Light Energy" who wished to experience Himself/Herself many times over, and therefore sent out "sparks" of Himself/Herself throughout the universes He/She had created. These little sparks were perfect also, as God, yet began to experience so much diversity and distractions in the three-dimensional, material worlds that they began to lose their connection to, and awareness of, God or Source—God and His/Her creation had become separated.
>
> A further analogy would be the scenario of a scuba diver descending too deeply to the ocean floor seeking a treasure. The treasure is so alluring that he pushes deeper and deeper until he loses all communication with his team on the surface. He becomes scared, confused, and disoriented. His lifeline is damaged.
>
> The diver, in essence, has not changed, and his team is still awaiting and supporting him. His confusion and sense of separateness changes entirely his perception of himself, his environment, and his sense of purpose. He becomes afraid. He feels insecure and all alone. Soon his verbal contact is restored and all is back to normal. His confidence is restored.
>
> We are the sparks of God, of Source, sent out as reflections of Him/Her into the material universe. And like the diver, we have lost our contact with our Source, in part because we have encased ourselves deeply in the material world over a long period of time. We perceive ourselves to be an infinite number of things, but unfortunately we've lost our sense of being the Divine spark of our original Creator.

We have learned to identify only with form and the three-dimensional, material world around us. The most serious of our misconceptions is that of our sense of separateness—separateness from our true Source. There are many byproducts of this illusion: fear, feelings of inadequacy and imperfection, egotism, experiencing lack, etc., just to mention a few.

Like the diver, if we can simply make contact again, our lives will come together—we will remember our original purpose, receive abundance, and feel connected with all of life. And, as with the diver, *we must ascend and consciously reconnect with Source. This reconnection is the basis for all spiritual paths.* If we're too entangled with materialism and the three-dimensional illusion, we cannot get a clear connection to our High Self or our higher potentials. Without this clear connection, we all too often accept disease and imperfection as being normal. *Perfect health is normal!*

When we do reconnect with our essence, our Divine spark, we will realize completeness, and our lives will reflect the great potential that was always been there: our wholeness, which manifests as love, light, and Divine power. We all truly possess these Divine qualities—they are our birthright!

This reconnection to Source is the key to everything of any value in our lives, including our health. Aligning with our own essence opens us to the vast inner, multidimensional energies that have always been available to us. These energies can inspire, create, heal, and bring love and joy into our lives, and more! Anyone seeking improved health must at least acknowledge this Greater Self and the greater potentials that accompany it.

The Effects of Thought and Emotion

Not all health problems relate necessarily to lessons that we need to learn. When we're not in tune with our higher potentials, then over time we manifest imperfections in our bodies through negative and unclear thinking, along with discordant emotions. Our bodies will eventually reflect, or, mirror all of our thoughts and feelings, whether they are positive or negative.

We've all met people who had very negative attitudes, and their face, posture, or general poor health reflected precisely their poor outlook on life. Conversely, it is rare that an individual with a clear mind and a positive outlook on life possesses a sickly body. In those rare cases, the soul has established a deeper lesson to be learned, for reasons that are usually beyond our human understanding. Sometimes it's simply to teach others through example.

There is a primary rule or law that should always be the foundation for all spiritual and metaphysical studies. It's understanding and application in the arena of healing is critical.

Energy follows thought.

Energy, whether it be purely mental, purely emotional, or even physical, will follow each and every thought we have. The more we think on something, the more energy or fuel we are feeding that thought. This is exactly why positive-thinking techniques and schools emphasizing the power of thought work so well.

In no other arena than that of health and healing is this law so important and so powerful. Our body is our temple—the housing, if you will, of our mind and emotions while we transit through our life. This body receives the energy our mind and emotions are putting out twenty-four hours a day.

Our physical body hears the thoughts and feels the emotions we are sending out. It does not distinguish between right or wrong, nor does it distinguish between conscious and subconscious thoughts, though the messages might be different. It receives and reflects each and every impulse our mind and emotions send out. Our subconscious is more powerful in its effect because it is always at work, mostly without our conscious awareness.

Healing involves the movement of energy. We are made of energy. We think with energy. We feel with energy. Health and vitality can manifest only when the energies are aligned, balanced, and working in harmony with the Soul.

This is why some of the more recent mental techniques of visualization work so well. For example, if an individual sends pure light energy and thoughts of love to his or her own body, each and every cell feels the pure, positive upliftment, and almost any ailment can be resolved and healed. Numerous terminal illness cures have been documented that prove this to be true. In Chapter III we'll look at more specific examples and how anyone can create their own positive thought pattern to help heal themselves in mind, body, and emotion.

Energy follows thought. If anyone chooses a spiritual or metaphysical path, learning only a portion of the power and usefulness of this law would provide them tremendous growth and power. *As a corollary to this law, in the healing arts, as in all of life, we are limited only by our imagination and our faith.*

You Can Heal Your Life by Louise Hay (Hay House, 1987) is an excellent self-help healing book that provides a tabular listing of many ailments and the probable cause of each. All of the causes revolve around imperfect thought and emotional patterns. The book is excellent in providing an affirmation that sets up the appropriate thought and/or emotional pattern to correct each ailment.

In positive-thinking schools, the essence of success is mentally picturing an outcome and then believing and feeling it to be a reality. With practice, and of course faith, success comes, and each success builds on the other, until the process becomes a way of life.

We can heal our bodies in precisely the same manner. We can visualize the perfect condition and energize that thought with positive, joyful emotions and feelings, then watch the process unfold. This is obviously an oversimplification, but the process parallels the already-proven schools of positive thinking.

This entire process revolves around the theme of energy. Thoughts are energy, emotions and feelings are energy, and our bodies are made of energy. Thoughts are the most subtle, then, by order of density, the feelings and the physical body. *Over time, subtle energy is the most powerful. This is why any change in our life must begin with a change in our mental attitude.*

Our mind is the director of our consciousness. It is comprised of subtle energy fields that consciously and subconsciously direct our body in an infinite variety of ways. We can consciously *will* the body to get up and walk across the room, or perhaps go to the track and run six miles. History has shown that those who believe strongly enough can use their *mind* and their *will* to perform extraordinary physical feats. This use of will, along with the mind, is the primary element that is employed for all healing, especially self-healing.

In many other ways, our mind can direct energy to our body and affect its processes dramatically. Witness the myriad of stories and documentaries from the East that tell of yogis and masters controlling their breath, their pulse, and even their digestion and sleep. There is no doubt of the power that the mind has over the body.

In more subtle ways, our mind affects the energetics of the body. When I first came into this field of study years ago, I wanted proof of some of the metaphysical concepts I was learning about, such as telepathy, the existence of the human aura, etc. I did a test with one friend who was especially telepathic. I would take five or six playing cards in my hand, and visualize one strongly in my mind. My friend, not knowing any of them, could tell me which card I was thinking of nearly four out five times.

A more meaningful test relating to healing was a test I did with another friend who saw the auric field around a person very clearly. I would visualize a color coming into my body and filling up my entire energy field. My friend could see my aura—nearly 100 percent of the time she would see the very color I was mentally bringing into myself. A similar realization of this phenomenon takes place when I work with my clients. I will be mentally and spiritually bringing in a color, filling up my client's energy field with it for healing purposes, when suddenly the person will say, "I see so much blue (or whatever color I'm working with) in my mind's eye." When I let them know that I also am working with the same color, they are quite surprised, and sometimes overwhelmed. There is no doubt that the mind affects greatly our energy field.

Subconsciously our mind is directing our body to breath and pump our heart, which in turn circulates our blood, which in turn takes oxygen and nutrients to all of the cells in the body while carrying the toxins to the kidneys. Our subconscious mind performs hundreds of tasks similar to this for our entire lives. This level of our mind is extremely helpful and very powerful as well when it comes to self-healing.

Subconscious means "below conscious." Just below our conscious mind lie a tremendous amount of subconscious thought patterns, many of which we have never processed consciously, but unless we are completely clear of all of our past, including childhood patterns or relationships, conflicts, etc., our subconscious mind remains cluttered and not clear to do its best work. Remember, our body does not judge whether a thought is right, wrong, good, bad, etc.—it receives all thought with equal measure. Consequently, as the subconscious is working at governing our bodily functions, it may be hindered by the suppressed, buried thought patterns lurking there. *Our health is directly affected by the state of our subconscious mind.*

Additionally, nearly all of our thoughts have a feeling attached to them. It is rare that we can have a clear thought, void of a feeling or emotion connected with it. This is because we are such emotional creatures, possessing logical, and many times critical minds. Our minds and emotions are delicately interconnected.

As a little test of this connection of thought and feeling, think of a person you know—not necessarily a friend or enemy, maybe a coworker—and look closely at your thoughts when you picture them. Are you absolutely empty of feeling about this person? Does he or she conjure up some type of emotion, positive or negative? Now imagine if that person and you had a conflict at one time or another. The feelings would circle like vultures around the thought of that person. Because of the way emotions are connected to thought, we must always keep our feelings positive at all costs. Remember that energy follows thought.

Summary

Let's summarize some valuable points:

♦ It is very important that our subconscious mind not contain suppressed thoughts and feelings that feed energy to areas in ways of which we're not aware. *We must take ownership of all thought and feeling—conscious or subconscious. We cannot manifest health and perfection in our life when we're out of control of our thought and emotional pattern.*

♦ It is rare to have thoughts without feelings, and feelings are the fuel behind the thought. Feelings and emotions build upon the thought and give it energy—remember that *energy follows thought.* This energy gives the thought power. *When we understand this law and how to apply it, we can begin to fuel positive thoughts with emotions of love and joy and happiness that will bring the spark for self-healing.*

♦ Our subconscious is at work all of the time. *Once we set up a positive thought form, fueled with positive energy, the subconscious will begin sending positive, healing energy to the body all of the time, without our conscious effort.*

♦ Equally as important to understand is that the opposite is true: *negative thoughts and emotions feed the wrong type of energy to our bodies all of the time, day and night. Fear, suppressed anger, criticism, intolerance, etc., feed negative energy to our bodies right down to the cellular level. Negative emotions are the biggest energy "drainers" we can have because of the extreme power our emotions possess. In all healing, never energize the problem—only the solution.*

It's not what a man puts in his mouth, but what comes out of it that makes him what he is.

Planetary and Cosmic Energy

Energy exists everywhere in the universe. We see it at work in all aspects of our lives. It sometimes manifests itself in very subtle ways, but nevertheless, there is nowhere one could go and not experience energy at some level if one were sensitive to the more subtle levels.

On our planet there exist vast energy fields and patterns. Some we have created over long periods of time, and some reach us from within the planet itself. These latter energies are out of our control. Some energies work to enhance our power, our life force, while others work against our internal harmony and personal energy fields. The latter forces tend to deplete our energy by disrupting, damaging, and draining our individual energy system.

We all have experienced the wonderful sensation of peace and serenity we feel after a day in a park, near the ocean, or in the mountains. We feel refreshed and rejuvenated from absorbing the fresh air, sunshine, and the grandeur and harmony of nature. The natural settings of our planet function with processes and energies that work in harmony with each other. There are actually powerful, harmonious waves of energy existing in these natural settings, and we can receive much healing and rest by absorbing these waves and taking time to harmonize with them. Our natural state is one of health and harmony, and consequently our body craves this type of environment at times. Our body knows that these natural waves will aid in the healing process, and help restore our lost vitality. In reality all energy expresses as waves—some are simply more harmonious and beneficial to us than others.

Unfortunately, the opposite effect can sometimes be felt, such as driving a car in a large city with all of the traffic problems, car emissions, loud noises, crowds, negativity from others,

etc. Stressful jobs, demanding schedules, and unhealthy relationships all add to the breakdown of our personal energy field
as well. Additionally there are many negative energies that
affect our health and well-being but are just beyond our normal awareness—we simply don't notice them until it's too late!

The energies we're discussing may originate from a local area or the environment such as a house, a room, or an office, or they may orig-inate from another country, another planet, or even another dimension. We will probably never totally understand the source and cause of some these energy movements, but we must always be attentive to them so that we can either avoid them, or simply stand aside and let them flow. That's not to say that all unseen energy is necessarily nega-tive. There are clearly positive ener-gies around us as well, as can be witnessed in the healing processes

> *We must be aware as much as possible of the impinging effects of energy upon us. We cannot confront properly, or even avoid a negative or scattered energy, if we are unaware of it. In other words, if we don't know that there are cars on the road, we'll probably get hit by one!*

we are about to discuss. But our guards are needed for the
potential negative energies around us—the positive ones are
quite welcome.

Cycles and Forces

All of life moves in cycles; there is really nothing static in the
universe. The larger, vaster energy fields of the universe are no
exception. In many cases these larger cycles are the primal
cause for the lesser cycles of life on our planet. In the field of
healing, these cycles must always be considered. As an example,

simple feelings of low energy may just be a short-lived cycle of passing cosmic energy that will move through us quickly. Low-energy days can also be a sign that we need to rest and slow our life down a little, or they can offer us a time in which we can process our life, our condition.

Our bodies perform functions in cycles as well, from the purely biological cycle, as in the case of the twenty-eight-day menstrual cycle, to the astrological cycles of the moon and planets. These cycles, too, must always be considered as they affect greatly our moods and health.

Forces such as the astrological aspects just mentioned can be predicted somewhat, and we can utilize them to help our life force as well as to aid us in avoiding certain actions at certain times. Astrology has long been viewed as a Divine Science and can also assist in a general diagnosis when one's Sun sign, Moon sign, and ascendant is considered. Certain configurations tend toward certain health problems.

One does not need to know astrology to learn to heal and be healed, of course, but, like the understanding of anatomy, physiology, or biology, a general knowledge of the totality of our being is always helpful. For example, if an ailment such as asthma (respiratory) is common for a certain astrological sign or configuration, then most likely the patient has been dealing with this problem for many years, and it's unlikely to be a simple allergy or temporary condition. In this situation, deeper emotional issues and lessons may need to be looked at. Possibly the use of mental affirmations would be the best tool.

At grand levels, massive energy fields move through galaxies and universes affecting every particle in their path. To a certain extent we have little choice but to flow with these greater cycles and energies. As we proceed into the new millennium, the cycles and patterns of energy that are entering the field of Earth are increasing exponentially. We must learn to adapt quickly to change; *change is indeed the only constant.* It is no secret that we are experiencing tremendous changes in our global weather patterns. These shifts are the result and the physical reflection of energy pattern shifts at other levels. *As above, so below.*

Many problems we now face related to our individual and collective health can be attributed to the increased energy cycle Earth is now transiting. There are numerous perspectives as to the source and cause of this new energy, ranging from the "Photon Belt energy theory" to the return of the Kali Yuga 26,000-year cycle as described by the Indian philosophy. Other explanations include purely religious prophecies, and a God who is seeking revenge on mankind for our poor behavior and our sins. Other, more scientific perspectives include the shifting of the polar axis, the greenhouse effect, etc.

The source of the energy we are confronting, as well as how we respond to it, can only be processed and integrated through the filter of our personal perception. Whatever the real cause of the dramatic energy shifts Earth is experiencing, one need not look very far to see that there exists a massive increase in activity, both positive and negative, on the planet. Family counseling centers are backed up, drug and alcohol addictions are accelerating daily, violent crime is on the rise, dramatic disasters are becoming commonplace, on and on.

In basic physics, we know that "every action has an opposite and equal reaction." What we are seeing projected in our world is the reaction, or the effects of some "thing." Behind this "thing" is the original action or energy.

This increase in energy and these effects could be compared to the act of turning up the volume on your stereo. If you have very clear reception and a clear signal, increasing the volume makes this already-clear signal louder. If, however, the reception is poor and there is much static, increasing the volume also increases the static. This is the situation we have on our planet now. The volume is being turned up—the energy is increasing.

Some individuals are clear and therefore more energized in their life in positive ways. Others who are not clear, who possess psychological blocks, or much fear, or any number of distortions in their psyche, are experiencing amplification of these distortions. *The increase in energy is increasing our consciousness, our expression, regardless of what that consciousness represents.*

Another example is a pipe carrying water to the homes in a neighborhood. Under normal conditions the pipe has the ability to contain the water under specific operating pressures. However, if by accident someone increases the pressure of the pumps at the water source, the pipe would burst—and it would burst at the *weakest point*. We are witnessing our weaknesses being amplified, so to speak, and our vulnerabilities are coming to the surface now that cosmic energy is being transmitted to us more rapidly. We are becoming more vulnerable in our weakest areas. This is another important process to understand in the arena of the healing arts—individuals everywhere are being energized and are becoming more sensitive, and are therefore extremely delicate and vulnerable.

In a very real sense, individuals are being accelerated in their personal growth, and personal growth always gets reflected in the physical health and energy level. Changes in our thoughts, our belief systems, and our emotional patterns all eventually mirror themselves in our bodies. This is why at this time there are so many problems; accelerated growth and increased energy levels are making it difficult for our bodies to adjust and adapt. In previous time periods, energy levels reaching the

Earth were such that our physical bodies could easily adapt to our environment. But for all of the reasons mentioned above, our bodies are now having a difficult time of it.

The good news is there has never been a time on Earth where *personal growth could accelerate so rapidly*. With the tides of energy pulsating to Earth in increasing proportions, we have available to us opportunities unlike any before. We can surf these waves and elevate ourselves, or we can sink further into darkness and suffocate our life forces. It's simply a matter of choice.

In the field of healing, there are boundless potentials and possibilities available as never before. Remember that healing means to "make whole." This is the exact parallel of our personal growth pattern, the path back to wholeness. At this time, we need to allow ourselves, as healers with healing consciousness, to be propelled to greater heights of *energy, love, light, and spiritual guidance*—it's literally an opportunity of a lifetime!

Energies and events on our planet, even at great distances, can have effects on us. Our personal energy fields have a great ability to detect these, though sometimes below the threshold of our conscious awareness.

All is energy. When a natural disaster levels a city or country somewhere around the globe, we sense it. The emotional energy released from this kind of event is tremendous. There have been many cases in which individuals have actually felt odd or even sick, only to find out later that a major earthquake took place at the same time somewhere else on the planet, thousands of miles away.

As multidimensional beings, we have the sensory apparatus to pick up on all of these events and energies. In Chapter II we'll look at this multidimensional aspect of ourselves more fully, but for now, just be aware of this sensitivity that you possess. Fortunately we all have built-in filters so that we're never really bombarded with all of these energies at once.

With all of the energies and frequencies we must contend with in our daily lives, attempting to process consciously those energies of other beings who are thousands of miles away, along with the multidimensional energies within us, would be a hopeless chore. Without a filtering system, the information would sometimes be far too much for us to process within the limitations of our human brain!*

At the other end of the spectrum, we have positive energies that are affecting us, including those of the thoughts of our friends and loved ones. Sending loving thoughts to others provide healing, nurturing, and positive energy at unconscious levels. It's no secret that there is tremendous power in groups as well, or what is sometimes called *group energy*. Tremendous healing has resulted in this type of focused work, where groups form and open themselves to powerful healing energy, and direct that energy with positive intent.

> *Each and every action, including thoughts that we emanate, return in equal measure to their source. It is the law of our Universe.*

The power of group energy is not simply the number of people in the group, but increases by the "square" of the number of people in the group. For example, the power of four people is: 4 x 4 = 16, and so on. Groups provide a setting for Spirit to manifest, as long as the intention is proper. "*Where two or more are gathered in My name, there I Am.*"

---

* When this does happen, many forms of psychosis manifest. Traditional psychology does not recognize these other dimensions, and therefore is limited in the diagnosis and treatment of many psychotic patients who have opened their energy fields to the various multidimensional energy fields too quickly.

We must all be on our guard and discourage any type of negative talk or discussion. There's plenty to talk about in our present time period besides someone else! Besides, more often than not, what we see in others is a mere reflection of ourselves.

Fortunately for all of us, *the law of cause and effect keeps all of these energies in a dynamic balance.* Otherwise there would be no peace or stability, and chaos would be the order of the day.

With all of this said, planet Earth can provide tremendous personal healing for anyone with the proper intention and openness. What energy field, what consciousness, would know better just precisely what your body, mind, and emotions need than that of Earth? Mother Earth has raised, nourished, supported, and nurtured billions of life streams before us. It is a vast consciousness that *knows* our individual and group needs. Earth knows us. We are *cells* in Earth's body.

> *The Earth knows your needs, your consciousness, your energy. The Spirit of the Earth is one of the greatest of all facilitators for healing.*

At very deep levels of our consciousness we know and understand Earth's dynamic energy field. It is similar to ours, yet obviously exists on a very large scale. Earth is growing and expanding in a similar manner, as we are. In an attempt to envision just a glimpse of this magnificent consciousness of Earth, let's do another visualization.

Imagine for a moment that you are the central Spirit, or the Soul, of planet Earth, and you are responsible for all life forms here—their protection and their entire support system. You are also responsible for the eventual destiny of each and every form of life on the entire planet. Not including the highly evolved, technical, and diverse group of life forms that you call the human kingdom, millions of others are under your stewardship as well—the mineral kingdom, the plant kingdom, the animal kingdom, the devic kingdom, and the integration of the various nonphysical life forms with those of the third dimension (our material world).

Witness the changing seasons and climates, the food chain, the birthing process, the ecological balances such as the oxygen and water system, the shifting of the magnetic poles, the temperature maintenance below the Earth's surface, just to name a few that are under your loving guidance. These are simple generalizations, but it doesn't take long to glimpse and appreciate just a fraction of the vastness and grandeur of the consciousness of our planet.

Around Earth's center, or Soul, revolve millions of electrons of life, all in their own personal orbits. These orbits are filled with all of the billions of lives that comprise all of the kingdoms in nature. Each life has a destiny, or at least what one might call a *probability* of a destiny. Each life affects the other, because Earth is just like an organism. All systems, cells, and atoms of an organism affect each and every other component of that organism. Earth is not without some flaws, however, but it is *grand, loving, and all-wise to the individual needs of each life form.*

The Spirit or Soul of Earth knows best what our personal energy field needs at any given moment. We are like tiny cells revolving and evolving in our own small orbits within Earth's beautiful field. Viewed as a total organism (Earth), we are integral cells (humans) within a system (humanity) that must work in harmony with other systems (mineral, animal, etc.).

We live and move and have our being within this great Spirit called Earth. Along with all of the life forms here, we and the energy of Earth combine to form one grand body of life.

From the vantage point of healing, we have some exciting perspectives:

♦ *Earth will heal us if we ask for it* properly and align our energy and intention with Earth's energy. At the close of this chapter I have included a meditation which not only allows the healing energies of the Earth to enter your consciousness, but can aid greatly in anchoring and grounding your personal field.

♦ *The interrelationship of all of life on our planet;* since all of life emanates energy, we are affected by all life forms on Earth, whether we realize it or not.

♦ *Earth is an energy field,* and we are individual energies within this field. The energies of Earth itself are in harmony. Getting in touch with the Earth is getting in touch with the *energy of the Earth.*

♦ *Earth is a vast unit of consciousness,* the realization of which leads us to a greater appreciation of all large bodies (planets) of consciousness from an energy standpoint. This may even provide a greater appreciation of our Sun, the *nucleus* of the greater *atom* of our solar system, in which the Earth itself is an electron moving in its assigned orbit.

Taking this last point a step further, tremendous inner healing can take place as well by tuning into our Sun. Our Sun, the primary source of our life and sustenance on this planet, as well as all others in the solar system, radiates healing energies on many levels. The Sun is great for healing such aspects as internal organs, the nervous system, the skeletal system, or most any system or area of our life that needs it. The only limitation is our imagination and our openness. A Sun meditation is also included at the close of this chapter.

Going back to the opening discussion at the beginning of the chapter on energy and its definition, the only real way we know energy is through what we sense and experience through our faculties, physical or otherwise. *Energy is life. It is the essence behind all that we see, governing all that we experience, especially to the healer. Energy is the essence and the media for making whole.*

We've looked at a general perspective of human and cosmic energy as it relates to our psyche, to our health. It's important as healers to be aware of some of these *ethereal* energies in order to understand more of our current situation. However, a perfect energy pattern does indeed exist in our personal energy field. This pattern endures our every action, every thought, and lasts throughout a lifetime. By realigning with this pattern, joy, abundance, and health become once again a reality in our life. The following pages will outline some methods and processes that can help us reach that goal—*it is our birthright!*

The following is a good affirmation for energy and general well-being:

I am whole and perfect.
My energy is aligned with the harmony
of the Earth's energy,
I am balanced, I am energy, I am light.
I am, I am, I am, I am.

Healing Meditations

It's important in this meditation to focus on the energy of the Earth and the essence you feel when you touch into this energy. The real key is to believe and to be open. This is also a good step in beginning to work with subtle types of energy. Remember that by asking, "Ye shall receive."

Earth Healing Meditation

Remember that healing may be needed in a variety of ways: emotional, physical, financial, etc. Mother Earth can help you heal yourself in whatever area you choose to focus upon.

Find a relaxing, serene place for this meditation. Ideally this would be in nature somewhere—a woods, near a pond or creek, or simply outside in the fresh air. However, this meditation works anywhere and anytime. Get yourself relaxed and quiet, using a technique familiar to you. If you have not developed one, simply allow the body to relax as you nonjudgmentally follow your breath. Do not struggle with your thoughts or any jumbled emotions, but allow them to flow in and out as waves in the ocean, returning gently to your breath.

Bring your attention to a ball of white, radiant light located at the center of the Earth. Sense and feel the power and love emanating from this energy. From this center visualize a bright, golden ray of light radiating upward, through the Earth's crust and into your body. This golden ray is grounding and revitalizing.

Allow this energy of Mother Earth to enter through the base of your spine, or through your feet, and fill your entire body. Ask Mother Earth to assist you in grounding your energies. Ask that any and all energy not of your highest good be grounded back to Earth, back to its source. Feel yourself becoming grounded and anchored.

Alternatively, visualize a root system extending from the bottom of your feet and growing deep into the earth. Feel the essence and life force within the rich soil below you. Imagine this life force grounding your energies. Ask that any/all energy within you that's not of your highest good be grounded. Feel this process of grounding your energy begin, and stagnant, scattered energies leave your body through your new root system.

Ask for healing to flow from the central core of Earth, the ball of white light, to you. If there is a specific area needing healing, then ask specifically for healing energy to go there. Also ask Mother Earth to show you, in whatever form appropriate (intuition, a book, a doctor, etc.), how you can facilitate your own healing process. Maybe more time in nature would help, or maybe Mother Earth will bring a new book in your life that will trigger the appropriate steps for you. You will also be given direct healing energy from the Earth, proportionate to your openness to this process.

For a few moments, just relax and allow the essence of the Earth to enter your essence and begin to balance and heal your field. Mother Earth always knows the areas you need to balance the most, and just the exact way in which to do it.

Replacing the golden ray now is a ray of green, brilliant energy. This ray will assist in healing at all levels. Along with the golden ray, the green ray will also help energize your body at the cellular level and clear out all of the elements that are holding you back in your growth and in your cellular expansion.

Begin feeling this beautiful, Kelly-green energy entering and filling your entire body. It may help to imagine yourself under a showerhead, or under a magical waterfall in the woods, with beautiful, scintillating green, vibrant energy filling your body, mind, and emotions with healing energy. Feel each and every cell being bathed and rejuvenated in this energy. For a few moments simply be—let go of all thoughts. Even if you do not immediately feel this energy doing its magic, know that it is truly working.

With regular practice you will be able to tap into this energy no matter where you are located physically. Earth's energy knows no boundaries! With unlimited thinking, you can have unlimited healing.

Sun Healing Meditation

The Sun is the source of all life, or energy, in our solar system. It sustains life, not only here on Earth, but provides the all-encompassing life force and energy for all of the other planets as well. The Sun is a self-sustaining source of energy. It radiates its light, heat, and energy for millions of miles in all directions. Some refer to it as the "God" of our system.

We don't necessarily need to use the Sun for grounding, since our primary grounding energy is planet Earth, but we can tap into other, more refined energies that will heal our bodies and our energy fields. The Sun meditation is excellent for focusing on healing to the systems of the body.

As in the Earth meditation, it is extremely important to be as open and imaginative as possible.

Use the same grounding technique as in the Earth meditation above, allowing yourself to get grounded to Earth. Be sure that you are grounded, relaxed, and as free as possible from Earthly stress. Once relaxed, move into a state of mind that perceives the Sun as the Source of all energy and healing in our Solar System. Know that your body, mind, and emotions can be healed directly when you are open to these subtle energies of the Sun.

Choose a system in your body that you feel needs some healing energy: skeletal, nervous, digestive, immune, etc. Now visualize a vibrant purple ray of energy extending from the Sun to your body. Bathe your entire body in this deep purple river of energy. Imagine yourself in the center of an imaginary cylinder, and see this cylinder fill up with the purple energy.

Mentally ask the Sun for healing, then ask that the system that needs healing receive the focus of this energy. After a few moments, move to another system or area of the body, or allow this energy to fill your emotional body. Just say, "Sun, I ask that you balance my emotions," or, "Sun, I ask that you balance and bring peace to my mind." Visualize a ray of healing energy extending from the Sun directly to your body.

With a little practice you will begin to feel these energies come to you, and you will experience the peace and healing that will follow.

Experiment with other colors such as green, violet, yellow, or gold. You will find there is no limit to the healing potentials that are dormant within you. If you are not a visual person, your intentions for a specific color will bring that color to your energy field. Whatever you can conceive in your mind, you can draw to you! Your intentions set up your receptivity. Grand and wonderful energy fields, from the Earth and Sun, are eager to assist you once you open to them and simply ask for their assistance. Enjoy!

II

The Nature of
Personal Energy

Now that we've taken a brief look at energy and how it
affects us, let's look at how it becomes personalized in
each of us.

We are one, yet we are all unique.

This Zen paradox is perhaps one of the greatest ones that
describes human consciousness. Spiritually we sense and *know*
that we are one, and sense a kinship with all of life. Yet, in our
human kingdom it is apparent that we are all very unique in our
personalities and expressions—we possess a unique, personal
identity. Underlying this identity are various energy patterns

Understanding the nature of personal energy will help us
understand the above paradox, but more importantly *will help us
as healers to understand the nature of illness and the condition of
the personal energy pattern that contributes to illness.*

Energy: East vs. West

Personal energy has been defined and quantified in a variety of ways in the field of healing. For example, the healers and philosophers of India talk about *prana*. In that culture, the belief is that all of our energy comes from prana, or tiny, invisible energy packets that exist all around us. We absorb it from the air we breathe and from the food we eat. The Indian schools break prana down into further divisions, but to them we essentially live and exist because of the prana which we ingest and assimilate.

The Chinese have a similar perspective of energy called *Chi.* When a Chinese acupuncturist inserts needles at certain points on a *meridian* along the body, it is to open up the flow of Chi along that meridian. This modality has been successful for thousands of years. It is based on this simple concept: keep the Chi (energy) flowing in the proper direction along the meridians that run throughout the body, and a person will remain healthy. Acupuncture has become quite popular here in the West. Westerners are rapidly opening up to many of these other, more natural healing methods that have proven to be effective for thousands of years in other cultures.

The Eastern cultures, in general, do not separate body and mind. They view them to be inseparable—one affecting greatly the other. Yoga and the slow-moving physical art/exercises of Tai Chi and Qi-Gong are prime examples of the way body and mind can merge. In the West we tend to separate body and mind, and have only recently come to realize the importance and power of this sensitive relationship.

The modern approach to energy has generally been the classical view of mechanical, chemical, or electrical energy. In traditional medicine, antibiotics are used to offset many ailments at the chemical and cellular level. Unfortunately, their treatments primarily address the symptom and not the cause. Our bodies reflect symptoms, while the cause lies at deeper levels of our consciousness at our *energetic level.*

That's not to underestimate the power or the appreciation of modern medicine, but only to look at the approach that much of it takes—it overlooks the energetics behind the symptom, or the cause behind the effect. For example, if one has a continual problem with ear infections, external medicines (antibiotics) induced into the body will temporarily treat the symptom, but the real cause may be a refusal to listen to others, or to self. When this cause is completely understood, the ear problems will go away. On the other side of the coin, if one were to break a leg, get to a doctor immediately! In all issues of health, there really is no substitute for common sense.

In the past ten years or so there has been much work and investigation here in the West into the existence of the human energy field or aura. The Russians were the first to show scientifically this existence through the use of Kirlian photography. This method awakened Western scientists to the real possibility of an electromagnetic and electrostatic field around the human body. Kirlian photography can actually capture the subtle energy field around living things, such as humans and plants.

Much more work has been done since then by such doctors as Dr. M. T. Morter, Jr., a chiropractor. He took the general philosophy and concept of the interrelatedness of the physical body and the electromagnetic counterpart and began a new technique, the Bio-Energetic Synchronization Technique (BEST). Out of his work came a number of profound realizations.

Perhaps one of the most interesting discoveries, and one that should have always been obvious, is this: *there exists around every single flow of current an electromagnetic field, and each and*

*every impulse and thought in our bodies produces such a field.
This is basic physics. Healing can occur through these fields. This*
is why spiritual healing occurs. *The alignment of these fields and
the balancing of the electromagnetic energy from a healer allow
the currents in the body to also become aligned and balanced.
The more focused and developed the healer, the better the energy
can be balanced.*

A similar healing effect is produced on our personal energy
when we spend time with nature, and our energy fields are
immersed in the harmonious and vibrant fields that exist
there. We've already discussed how nature is in harmony with
itself, and is especially powerful in a forest, near an ocean, or in
the mountains. The overwhelming power of the natural vibrations penetrate our personal energy pattern completely.

Energy Fields

Let's do a little review. In Chapter I, we said that the body pro-
jects or mirrors our thoughts and feelings over time. Looking
at the process from another vantage point, our thoughts and
emotions have energy and over time have powerful effects on
our body. This occurs through the medium of energy fields.

It doesn't matter which approach or definition of personal
energy you choose to endorse (prana, Chi, electrical/chemical,
or electromagnetic), the energy of your body has to be flowing
clearly and openly to achieve health. *When you are truly in tune
with your body, you will know which avenue to take toward perfect health. You will know the most efficient and long-term
modality that will heal your body. Additionally, therapies and
modalities may change from time to time, depending on the
changes in your energy field.*

We also mentioned in Chapter I that our energy can be
blocked in a number of ways, but mostly through negative or
wrong thinking and out-of-balanced emotions. We discussed

the concept of the Soul, the individual Divine essence, and that as Soul expressions, we have a physical body, an emotional body, and a mental body. Each one of us has our own unique expression, or *energy field*. Let's take this concept a step further into the arena of metaphysics.

Our Soul, or essence, chooses our parents and the conditions in which we can best serve our chosen lessons, and the best place that provides an environment for our highest good and growth potentials for our entire lives. We choose this situation for general points of growth, *but not everything is necessarily predestined. We set up prior to birth a probability of our life. We still have free will and cocreative powers to affect this probability for good or for whatever purpose we choose. This free will is a gift from Source.*

In the process of incarnating, we bring with us our specific DNA coding (with input from our parents) that determines our body type, our emotional tendencies, our mental abilities, our potentials, etc. This is actually a coding that our Soul carries with it that is transferred to our physical DNA structure. Additionally, we bring to our life all of our past experiences (though at subconscious levels), including our spiritual attainments. We bring also a subconscious pattern of the primary lessons we agree to learn during our life. This is reflected to some degree in the schools of astrology. Astrology, by the way, can provide a road map of the probability of accomplishments we may achieve in our lives, as well as our abilities and challenges. It can also help to plot our probable personality pattern and tendencies.

We are all born with certain lessons to learn, and until they are mastered, they will repeat themselves no matter where we may go or what we may do in our lives.

Conversely, one could argue that our emotional and mental tendencies are primarily determined by our upbringing. On the surface this is many times the case, but once our *garden of life* is examined and cleared, we find that we do indeed possess our own unique personality blend of body, mind, and emotion. Remember that we chose our early environment for a reason, whether it was karmic or to learn specific lessons, and we must take responsibility for our childhood, no matter how difficult that might appear. As long as we feel as if we are a victim, we will be bound and confined to all types of limitations.

A large arena of healing is devoted to the clearing of this garden or releasing the creations of past blockages. To understand who we are, and to understand our personal energy, we must be clear of childhood blockages, misconceptions, suppressions, fears, etc. Otherwise, we will never express our true self. These past blockages and traumas are what create the various filters that affect our perceptions—especially in close relationships. These perceptions, in turn, establish the subconscious baseline for all of our interpersonal communication and relationships.

Though this author is not a psychologist or a psychiatrist, these schools of counseling and self evaluation are nearly always essential in helping one along the spiritual path, or in the process of healing, at one stage or another. *The reason is that emotional blocks actually block and limit our physical energy. Mental misconceptions or limitations block our potentials. Remember that all thought and emotion are mirrored in our body, and that includes unclear, negative, rigid, or suppressed thoughts and feelings. These occur mostly at unconscious levels; they are the weeds in our garden of life.*

Psychology, in all of its aspects, such as its virtues of service and its accomplishments, does not generally address the spiritual or multidimensional levels. Only in rare cases will a practitioner step over the fence of traditional counseling and go into the depth of an individual. Psychology does not usually address our past life experience, the integration of our mind and body, nor does it address the energetics of our expression as we have been discussing. As in most of the traditional schools of medicine, psychology has its place, but it can only take us so far on our spiritual journey of understanding and of energy. Some psychologists today are indeed becoming more holistic in their approach. Ideally this will be a trend that will parallel the medical and chiropractic field in its broader approach to total health.

Body, Mind, and Emotion

Let's continue to examine who we are at the basic physical, emotional, and mental levels. Then we'll look at this structure in relation to our health and other levels of our being, including the etheric, astral, and the multidimensional self. Let's view our physical, emotional, and mental bodies as energies of expressions for our Soul.

Some of the following discussions cover these areas and may be a review of sorts for many people. The discussion is brief, and it's worth the time in order to appreciate our total identity and the wonderful temple we live in.

The Amazing Physical Body

In our three-dimensional, material world, we are most commonly identified by the uniqueness of our personal form—our physical body and appearance. Our size, shape, color, and especially our facial features provide us with an identity in this physical world in which we live. For mass consciousness, this means of identification is the only one available at this time. Could I see a photo ID, please?

As evolving, aware beings, it is critical to sense the *energetics* of a being or of a patient requiring healing, more than their physical qualities or characteristics. However, we'll take an overview of our wonderful physical body, which has developed over millions of years. In reality we'll look at it from the healer's viewpoint, in order to more completely understand our composite personal energy and how to heal it.

We've already emphasized how our physical body reflects our inner state of being. We choose a family with the type of DNA structure that will provide us the necessary form to live in, and one that will help us accomplish our predetermined mission and lessons.

Many of our lifelong habits are learned from our family at a very early age. For example, many of our tendencies and tastes for food are set in motion by our parents, teachers, and those close to us when we are young. However, as we mature and get in touch with who we are, what we learned to eat, as well as how much and how often, is no longer the best for our body. Good health is not totally dependent on diet, but one's health can be dramatically affected by diet.

What is a good diet for one may not necessarily be a good diet for another. Each one of us must listen to our body and feed it what we feel it needs, along with drinking plenty of good, clean water. Diet is mentioned here because all too often a health practitioner tries to force a better diet on someone, when in truth the *spiritual, mental, or emotional body is the area of real need for healing and balance.* If you are struggling with your current diet, know that a proper diet for each of us will fall into place naturally when the other areas are changed.

A physical treatment alone, whether it is diet, exercise, rest, outside activity, chiropractic treatment, antibiotics, or other methods is usually not enough to restore complete health in a serious or chronic condition. In fact, *treating solely from the physical level is one of the least powerful approaches in most cases.* That's not to say that any one of the above treatments won't prove to be extremely helpful, but in nearly all recoveries, the mental and emotional healing supplements and actually drives the other treatments.

In descending order of power, we have: the spiritual, the mental, the emotional, and then the physical level. In generating self-healing and self-awareness, we should begin with the more subtle levels, and the denser levels will follow suit. Ideally, we should energize all levels at once in order to bring balance and perfect health into our lives more quickly. The single most common cause of illness in the Western countries is stress. This factor and all stress-related activities must be seriously and closely looked at on the road to complete recovery.

> *The more subtle the energy, the more powerful it is over time.*

"When we don't know who we are, everything we eat affects us. When we know who we are, nothing that we eat will affect us." I don't know who made this statement, but it summarizes very well the point about diet. When we are clear, balanced, and in harmony with all of our levels, diet is not nearly as important, nor are many of the physical plane treatments. What is important is the *energy flow and/or energy blocks that the physical body is dependent upon for vitality.* What we eat is certainly important to our health. It's simply a matter of balance and moderation.

A person may fast for two to three days and rid himself/herself of muscle spasms or poor digestion. This is an excellent approach to many ailments of the body, since it *allows* the body to *regenerate itself in its normal process.* However, if the cause of the spasms or poor digestion is not handling a stressful job well, or not confronting personal issues in a relationship, the ailments will return.

There are infinite examples of physical treatments that work, but only for a short time *unless the underlying cause is considered*. Looking at the complete person for the cause of an ailment has become known as *holistic* treatment—the examination of all aspects of our lives and possible causes of a disease or ailment, not just the treatment of the symptom.

Many common afflictions, such as colds and flu-like problems, are caused by a combination of stress, which weakens the immune system, and the actual exposure to a virus. Most common viruses are handled by our body quite well when our immune system is in proper working order. There are very good herbs on the market that help strengthen our immune system, but a lifestyle with minimal stress is required in order to keep our immune system strong.

The physical body is a wonderful vehicle. It is an organism with interworking systems that operate unconsciously, and always in our best interest. The role of diet is only one example of purely physical approaches that work only partially. Another physical approach, medication, in many cases suppresses the underlying cause of a problem because it essentially focuses on the symptom: pain, stress, spasms, depression, etc. In many cases medication works counter to the natural systems of the body, such as the immune system and the nervous system, by depriving them their natural process. Thus, medication is much like a crutch.

Overdependence on medication is a serious problem in our Western culture. We spend millions of dollars each year trying to hold the illegal drug problem in check, but what of the millions of dollars we spend legally on Valium and many other legal drugs? What about the millions spent on antibiotics that are overused and that destroy the natural bacteria in our digestive tract? There is a time and place for most medications, but overuse and dependency on some legal drugs is appalling, especially when one considers that these medications are being *prescribed* by trained medical doctors who often ignore the long-term side effects.

Chiropractic

Chiropractic adjustments help the body heal itself by keeping the major portions of the spine (the vertebrae) in alignment. This allows the natural flow and process of the nervous system to keep the organs in proper working condition. As such, it is great preventative medicine as well as a healing tool. However, one setback with this modality is adjusting the spine when adjacent muscles are in a spasm. The realignment may help temporarily, but unless the adjacent soft tissues are relaxed, the spine will often be pulled out of place again. We must always keep looking for the cause, no matter how popular the treatment may be.

Some newer techniques used by chiropractors focus more on the cause of the misalignment rather than simply realigning or adjusting the spine. The BEST (Bio-Energetic Synchronization Technique) method, mentioned earlier in this chapter, is one that helps the body to detraumatize an area that causes the spine to get out of alignment. It looks at the motor nervous system and muscle group that is responsible for the misalignment and treats this causative area through nonforceful techniques. It helps to reset the body (nervous system, muscular system, etc.) to its natural state through energy balancing. Network Chiropractic addresses the body in a similar fashion.

Massage therapy supplements chiropractic care and other holistic approaches very well because it helps all of the applicable muscles to relax, releasing stress from the body. It soothes the mind and the emotions. At the physical level, massage also moves blood, which in turn moves out toxins that tend to get stored at the cellular level. Additionally, *massage moves energy.* As we'll see in the following pages, just outside our physical body is an *etheric energy pattern, and massage helps move the energy at this level as well.*

This etheric energy pattern holds our shape and provides most of the necessary energy channels for our physical body. Massage moves this energy and helps release blocks because (and remember, *all is energy*) we have such a force of energy in our hands. When one is placing their hands on another, the massage process is much more than just physical. Our hands possess intense energy, which interpenetrates the energy of the physical body and into the etheric levels. Therapeutic massage is relaxing and helps integrate our various energy levels. This is one example of a physical treatment that works well because it taps into so many layers of our being. It goes beyond the physical level.

Meditation for Health

Meditation is also excellent for our body, as well as our mind and emotions because it allows the body to relax naturally. We'll look more into this process in Chapter III.

I am whole and integrated on all levels of my being,
I am using my body as a perfect temple
for my expression.
I see my body in perfect health,
I am perfect on all levels.

The physical level is the most dense and has the lowest vibration of all our various levels—no offense, but even if you believe yourself to be beautiful physically, that beauty is only a small portion of who you really are. Just above this level in frequency is the etheric level. This is the pattern that determines your body shape, and it keeps energy (vitality) moving through your body. At birth the etheric template provides the mold in which your body is shaped. Each component of the physical body has a counterpart in the etheric body. This is important knowledge for a healer, especially when removing blocked energy.

Through a complicated process, your coding, including all of your past achievements at the soul level and your predetermined major lessons for this life, determines the parameters of your etheric template and subsequent physical characteristics. Any effective healing technique will utilize this etheric template that interpenetrates the physical body.

In order of descending vibration we have: spiritual, mental, emotional, *etheric*, and physical. The etheric is usually identified with the physical, and therefore most philosophies refer to our personality as the triad of mind, body, and emotion. All of these elements can be viewed as *frequency ranges*, or levels of vibration.

The etheric is affected strongly by our thoughts and feelings, and this is why our body is a reflection of these impulses. There are certain lines of force and energy patterns within the etheric level, as we ventured earlier. These are called meridians by the Chinese and those practicing Oriental medicine. The Chinese utilize these lines to treat patients through acupuncture, acupressure, and herbs. Once the meridian is opened through one of these techniques, the energy flows, and the problem is usually resolved very quickly. The physical body, being a reflection of the etheric, becomes whole and energized. Some advanced techniques can assist a person in need by simply visualizing the meridians being opened mentally.

Hands-on healers also use the etheric level, or *vital body,* as the primary avenue through which to heal. Good healers have another advantage: they are able to penetrate many other levels in the emotional and mental bodies. A good healer is able to tune into the soul of the patient and bring forth the required energy/treatment for him or her in that moment, regardless of what level the focus needs to be: physical, emotional, or mental. Much healing can be self-induced, as we shall see in the next chapter. Whether you are healing another or yourself, it's important in the beginning stages to direct your healing primarily to the etheric level.

Also at the etheric level is a system of chakras that works to bring energy to many levels of our being. This system is very powerful, and entire schools are devoted to healing through this chakra system. We'll take a closer look at this system at the end of the text. The theory of chakras and the application of acupuncture have been utilized in the Eastern cultures for healing for thousands of years. Another powerful system of healing at the etheric level uses geometric shapes such as the diamond and triangle. It is much newer, and we'll look at this technique and philosophy more closely in Chapter V.

Our physical body is an amazing organism. It is our *temple* as we transit through this physical dimension. Its health and well being are critical to our overall success and achieving our purpose in life. We've all had that wonderful feeling of being alive—of feeling the energy of life pulse through our physical body. There is absolutely no reason why we should not have this feeling all of the time—it is indeed our natural state of being.

With all of the new modalities in healing and the various techniques available to us, finding the proper one for yourself can be quite confusing. At one time the gulf between the new, holistic approaches and the longstanding medical field was quite large. But now that gap is closing, as each side of the polarity is gaining respect, however slowly, for the other. You must realize that not all techniques and methods will work as well for you as for someone else, and vice versa. Experiment with various arenas. Sometimes an alternative method is tried only as a last resort, but with a very successful outcome. Use your intuition as well. Sometimes you will have to *feel* your way through the process.

As in all areas of our lives, we must always use common sense. One may not need to visit a traditional doctor for a cold, a sore back, or even a chronic headache. Other modalities may work fine—but for any serious emergency, get to a trained and experienced doctor!

Our body reflects our inner state or condition. With only a little practice of positive thinking or affirmation (see Chapter III), you will begin to see changes in your appearance, your health, and the quality of all aspects of your life.

Emotions

Remember that emotions are a primary source of our fuel, *especially fuel for our thoughts*. A suppressed feeling or emotion, such as anger or frustration, blocks our physical energy, as well as clouds our true emotional expression. Distorted emotions also distort our thinking. It's like a rock or an object that gets stuck in a pipe, or perhaps a bird's nest in a chimney. The water in the pipe and the smoke in the chimney will still flow, but with much more difficulty.

Suppressed anger tends to block and slow down liver functions, while overemotionalism tends to affect the lungs. These are just two simple examples of how emotional blocks or imbalances eventually affect our body and our health. We'll look more closely at releasing these blocks in the next chapter, but we must first understand a little of how they got there. Sometimes it is more than a simple childhood hurt or simply a suppressed feeling.

What makes matters more interesting and what many modern practitioners in various healing fields do not endorse in their healing modality is the concept of past lives. When we incarnate we bring with us the coding that determines our current personality. This coding also carries with it our past-life memories, including personalities, relationships, experiences, etc. These memories, which are primarily subconscious, tend to overlap with our present life in ways we're not always aware of at the conscious level.

These past-life *overlays* may manifest as meeting someone that you feel you've known before, or having a type of handicap that you cannot rationally explain. They may even manifest as certain experiences or situations that continually repeat themselves in your life. This may be a lesson, which has come forth in the current time period, and *until it is learned thoroughly, it will continually manifest in your life in one form or another.* Remember that we agreed prior to incarnating to learn certain, major lessons.

> **We must take ownership of all of our feelings.**

In a similar manner as our childhood hurts, past-life hurts can affect our current-life pattern and relationships. These are sometimes harder to resolve, but often parallel our childhood hurts and suppressions. One example would be meeting a person with whom you would like to have a personal relationship, yet you are fearful of following through with it. Maybe all of your other relationships have been clear and positive, but this one perplexes you. It is quite possible that this person hurt you in the past life, or, in reality *you felt hurt* as a result of a relationship with this person, whether the person intended to injure you or not. To be clear and healed from this feeling, you must first take responsibility for it.

This is a major hurdle for many of us, especially if we are emotionally sensitive. Unless we do take ownership of our feelings, we'll continually suppress them, avoid them, or blame others for our condition. As long as we stay in this *victim* mentality, we'll remain limited. At some level we have all placed ourselves in the exact situation we are in at each and every point in our life. As soon as we take responsibility for our lives and each situation in which we find ourselves, new doors will open and old limitations will begin to vanish.

When we are in balance and clear at all levels of our being, past-life patterns and experiences have little effect on us. We simply confront and live through any experience as it comes into our life. The past-life issue is being brought to light because many times we struggle

> *Mastery of our personal energy can only be accomplished in the present moment.*

with our processing of a relationship or emotional issue that has no tangible connection to our current-life situation.

The varieties of these experiences that impinge on present-day life are infinite. *The key is remaining balanced and clear in the present time, and dealing with our personal life situations on a moment-to-moment basis.* When we can do this, while taking ownership of the situation where we've found ourselves, we will become masters. *No matter what our condition or state of being, and no matter how unfair it may appear, we must take responsibility for it.*

We may ponder the *future* and process our *past* experiences, but in the *present* moment lies the real opportunity to experience and express life. As far as our personal energy goes, the emotional body is the most powerful. It is our fuel and it is the filter that our thoughts must go through when sent to the body. This is an important point: *our emotional body tempers our thoughts directed to our body, whether they are sent consciously or unconsciously. The same principle applies in the healing of others.*

When we send thoughts to our body, such as, "I'm getting old," or, "I feel great," or, "I hate the way I look," the quality and intensity of our emotional state gives the thought its real power. Look at the thoughts you have about yourself. You may think you have a good self-image, but have you fueled your image with feelings of joy and love? Have you envisioned your body as youthful, joyful, and full of energy?

Emotions fuel our thoughts and "color" the condition of our body.

Remember we're discussing energy, not necessarily what society may view as a beautiful body. Forget weight, gray hair, etc. Judgments of these traits are established from an ego-centered consciousness. The real issue is being in charge of a healthy, energetic, alive, and happy physical body. This can only happen when we are housing a clear, calm, and joyful emotional body. To achieve total health, we must express through clear, calm emotions.

There are many schools and counselors who can facilitate our personal growth and the processing of our emotions. We won't look into this process at any depth here, but it is critical for us to individually take ownership of our emotional state.

It is ludicrous for one to say: "You made me feel this way." That is no different than a child saying, "He made me do it." Herein lies the essence of a key emotional challenge: *To maintain a childlike innocence, while taking adult ownership and responsibility for our feelings.*

Another challenge we humans have is to think clearly without an attached emotion. We have already looked at how our thoughts and feelings are interrelated. Most people cannot think without attaching an emotion or feeling to the thought. How many conversations do you have during the day in which the discussion is perfectly calm and void of all emotion? That's not to say that emotion is bad; emotions are obviously quite good and quite powerful. In fact, some schools of metaphysics say that we cannot become enlightened or *self-realized* unless we experience our full capacity to *feel.*

As we grow, mature, and evolve, our emotions, like our minds, become more and more refined. When it is sufficiently developed, our emotional body becomes a vehicle at our disposal to fuel our thoughts and open the doors of our *feeling* nature. We can and should always embrace the *feelings* of life, joy, and aliveness.

As healers, much of the real power we have comes through our emotions, or through this feeling nature. This energy fills our *auric field* (aura), and gives our feelings power and presence. We've all heard and been inspired by dynamic speakers and motivators. It's not the message, nor the mastery of the English language, as much as it is the emotional flavor that motivates us—the joy, the excitement, or the thrill of the message is what moves us. In a different setting, and for a different purpose, healers must also utilize their emotions. With an open and clear emotional body, the healer can bring forward powerful healing energy. Anything less, and the spiritual flow will not be at its fullest potential.

One final note on the emotional body as it relates to healing and health. We tend to feel through our solar plexus, the energy center in our stomach area. Unless we are extremely protected and cautious, this feeling center may pick up on energy external to us. In this regard, some individuals are more sensitive than others. The point is this: *we must take ownership of our feelings, but we may also be affected by those around us in subtle ways.* This is not the same as our previous example. In that example, we were blaming another for our actions: "He made me do it," for example. This arena deserves a closer look.

All around us are fields of energy, moving around at different frequencies. We *plug into* the emotional fields with an extension of our solar plexus. This usually happens when we are tired or our defenses are down. As we evolve, we become more and more sensitive to energy fields around us. This is good in the sense that we are more sensitive and expanded, yet not so good if we're not careful, because we may pick up energy that's not ours, and often energy that is not good.

As healers we must be aware that our patients may be carrying around much useless energy that doesn't belong to them— or us! Additionally, some people, including children, can hook into our solar plexus and actually draw out our energy. Even events on the other side of the world create emotional energy that we can feel or tap into unconsciously at times. In the truest sense of the word, we are all connected—through energy!

There also exist *energy pools* or pockets of energy. These pockets can be positive, negative, or neutral. When an individual is depressed, for example, he or she will usually attract more of the same type of negative or depressing energy from this pool. This is the *Law of Attraction* at work.

This law is basically self-explanatory and is the essence of the concept of "energy follows thoughts." We draw to us the type of people, things, or experiences that we *vibrate* with. Simply by living on Earth we are challenged to protect ourselves and not draw upon some of the negative pools of energy that have built up over thousands of years. The key is to be positive and to continually keep our energy level up. When our energy is flowing outwardly, nothing will penetrate it. It would be like trying to force water up a waterfall.

Like attracts like.

♦

When our energy is positive, we can only draw positive energy to us.

The law of attraction can and should work to our advantage. As we gain momentum with a positive attitude toward ourselves and with our life, we draw to us these same positive energies. We attract positive, constructive events and individuals to us that support our belief system and supplement our life. *Each and every event in our life occurs for a reason, and the more positive and meaningful our life becomes, the more we attract this type of experience to us. We become the cocreators of our world, as we were meant to be.*

There are many types of positive pockets of energy that we can draw upon. Healers, architects, and fiction writers, among others, receive much of their inspiration from these types of energy reservoirs.

Of all of the areas of healing, releasing emotional blockages are the most powerful. Because of the power of human feelings, these locked or blocked emotions can prevent entire organs from functioning, drain away all of our energy, or even be the primary cause of terminal illness. This is the reason we've spent so much time discussing the emotional nature.

When one is healing another, it is important to attempt to get a general sense of the emotional nature and current status of the individual. Emotional blockages are often established during one's youth and therefore may require many sessions to release. Sometimes only deep laughter or deep crying will release such emotional scars. Through the *Law of Love*, all issues can be fully released, forgiven, and transmuted.

It may sound somewhat like *pie in the sky*, but love can consume and transmute all limitations. *True love* of self and others transforms and forgives, and in that *flame*, all limitations are lifted. If techniques and philosophy fail, simply *love yourself completely*. The emotional body will be healed beyond your greatest expectations!

Mind, the Director of Consciousness

Our brain is a very complex organ. Not even our most advanced scientists completely understand how it works. A consensus is rapidly forming, even among the scientific community, that there is a *mind* or mental *body* that is separate from this physical brain. There are many ways of viewing and exploring the mind. Let's look at a few.

In our everyday lives we use more of our *left brain*, or logical thinking process. When we have ideas or we are creating, such as an artist, we are using more of our *right brain*, or the creative side of the brain. In an ideal world, these two aspects are in balance with each other.

At a somewhat higher frequency are other levels of mind that some refer to as *superconscious*. At these levels, the left and right brains (energies) are in balance. Higher mathematics, architectural design, inventions, divine sculpture, and classical music are a few examples of this higher level. At this higher frequency or mental plane, *intuition* is also available to us.

These higher aspects of the mind are actually aspects of what we previously discussed as *Soul essence*. This is effectively a direct overlap where the spiritual and the physical dimensions intersect: *the higher, spiritual mind*. In other words, when we are using our spiritual mind, we have successfully brought forth the spiritual realm to our physical awareness.

Another way to view our mind is by dividing it into three areas: conscious, subconscious, and superconscious. The conscious mind is what we use daily as mentioned above. The subconscious mind works just below our consciousness and is affected greatly by it, as discussed in Chapter I. Our conscious mind can direct some of our bodily actions, but not all—it is our subconscious mind that is always at work, sending continual messages and directions to our body.

Our conscious and subconscious minds overlap in a number of ways, such as in our dreams, or in our power to consciously program the subconscious and the control of certain functions of the body, such as breathing. Over time our conscious, repetitive thoughts set up patterns in our subconscious that run like continual movies to our body, twenty-four hours a day. This is why affirmation and positive-thinking techniques work so well—they set up patterns that repeat themselves subconsciously and program our bodily systems in new behavioral patterns and habits. These patterns can create tremendous healing in our bodies, even affecting us at the cellular level.

The superconscious mind is actually an aspect of our Soul or High Self. It is that portion of the mind we use the least at this point in our human evolution. This aspect of our consciousness is responsible for those flashes of intuition, or genius, that we've experienced at times and it provides us the higher knowledge and wisdom of the spiritual worlds. *To get in touch with this superconscious aspect within us, we must go through the subconscious.* That is why so many people on a conscious spiritual journey tend to process so many personal issues. They are opening up to the superconscious mind, which overlaps the subconscious. To use our superconscious aspects, we must be very clear at the subconscious level. All memory, including past-life experiences, is accessed through our subconscious.

Any subconscious pattern not recognized consciously must surface and be processed and released in order for the super-conscious to flow clearly. It's a similar process as distilling water. We apply enough heat to the water so that it evaporates and leaves behind all of the unnecessary elements. These elements may be required in another process or application, but tend to *muddy* the waters. Our subconscious may muddy the conscious mind if not dealt with completely. With a muddy conscious mind, we cannot experience the superconscious mind and its qualities.

It is really quite simple: *processing personal issues helps to release blockages and old patterns in the subconscious. The clear-er the subconscious, the easier and clearer is the use of our con-scious mind, as well as the access to our superconscious mind.*

Keep in mind that our physical brain is not our mind. It is the physical counterpart of the thought process. It is essential-ly like a radio. For example, when we turn on our radio, we adjust the volume and more importantly, tune in a station we like. The radio, like our physical brain, must be in good work-ing order to get a clear station, or in our case, the mental images. Our physical brain must be in good working condition in order to tune in or think clearly on whatever subject we wish. *The brain is the vehicle for our mental expression. It has the potential to tune in to an infinite variety of mental fields of thought and creativity.*

Mental stress creates many problems in our society. We overload the conscious mind to the point of exhaustion, and then wonder why we are always tired, irritable, or sick. Remember that repetitive, conscious thought patterns tend to set up subconscious thought patterns that send messages to our bodies around the clock. When we are overstressed, we are sending scattered, unwanted messages throughout all of our body.

When we feel mentally stressed, we get frustrated because we are tired and out of balance. We are unable to function in a clear, balanced fashion. In this state we tend not to enjoy any sort of recreation (treat ourselves emotionally), and many times we ignore our physical body (proper rest and exercise). Our waking, conscious mind is primarily what is required for most daily tasks, but it is not designed for twelve-hour shifts at a computer, or five-meeting days, followed by work at a part-time job in the evening.

The conscious mind is our three-dimensional tool for much of our thinking in our daily life. It should never be overloaded to the point of physical breakdown and exhaustion. As with our physical body, it needs rest, exercise, and recreation. Needless to say, good health and balance in our life is dependent on a clear, balanced mind.

In summary, it really doesn't matter how we break down the elements of our mind, or how we perceive it. The mind is a multidimensional tool for accessing thought and directing that thought energy into the world. That world includes, of course, our physical body.

Etheric Level

We alluded to the *etheric body* earlier, and much of the healing that a hands-on healer provides occurs at this level. It is our template or pattern upon which the physical form is molded.

Many diseases can be cured by making this body perfect again, provided of course that the soul is in agreement.

The etheric body, like the emotions and the physical body, is affected tremendously by thought. It is also affected greatly by our emotions, and in some cases is even affected by physical activity, since the etheric and the physical plane overlap. Most people who begin to see auras, the energy field around a person, begin by seeing this etheric body. It is most easily seen just above the shoulders, or around the head or hands.

Acupuncture works well because of lines of force or meridians that run through the etheric body. The needles (sometimes pressure or visualization) open up these lines of energy when they are blocked, thereby opening up the physical blockages. As we discussed, Prana and Chi are similar definitions of energy units, and they are processed and assimilated at the etheric level first from the air we breathe and the food we eat.

If you hold your hands about three to four inches from each other, palms facing, you will most likely feel the warmth of the energy they are emitting. You are sensing your etheric field. It's also fun to do this exercise with someone else. This energy field that is located in the center of your palms is the primary focus of energy one uses to heal with. Whenever you place your hands on yourself, or on another, you are sending energy waves deep into the body. This is another reason why massage therapy works so well. The next time you meet someone and shake hands, try and sense their energy. Can you sense the quality of the energy from their hands? Is the energy cold? Warm? Strong? Weak? The energy from one's hands is a great measuring stick in determining the general type of energy that a person carries around. After all, their energy field is truly who they are!

The Chakra System

There are many books that cover in great detail the chakra system and how to heal through it. Tremendous healing and balancing can take place through these energy vortices, or *wheels* of force.* There are seven major chakras and twenty-two minor chakras in the body. Most healers focus on the major seven.

A chakra is a spinning vortex, or wheel, of energy. It is shaped like a spinning top, with the bottom, pointed end near the surface of the body. Chakras extend outward from the body approximately four to six inches. The chakras are anchored in the etheric field, just above the physical field from a frequency perspective. What many don't understand is that they are multidimensional, because they also penetrate astral, mental, and spiritual dimensions. The seven major chakras are connected to the primary glands, as well as to other major organs of the body. As we evolve, each of our chakras becomes more active, but more importantly, they become more and more refined. From one perspective, we have another definition of spiritual growth: *spiritual growth is the opening and refinement of all chakras.*

Eastern philosophy tells us there is a dormant energy at the base of the spine where the first, or base, chakra is located. As we open up spiritually, this energy, the *kundalini* force, rises through the spine, opening each chakra as it ascends. Enlightenment to many of the Easterners was simply the opening of the kundalini and the subsequent opening of all the chakras. The kundalini force is said to have its origin deep within the Earth itself.

One difference between the chakra system and the Chinese meridians and acupuncture is that the energy comes into the

---

* For the purposes of this text, we'll just take a quick glimpse at this system. There is much information available that discusses the chakras in great detail.

chakras as spiritual energy from other dimensional frequencies. In other words, our Soul can direct energy to the chakra system, or to a specific chakra directly. Chakras are also greatly affected by sound and color. This is the reason mental color baths and harmonious music help us so much—they are bringing balance to the chakra system. Nature is also a tremendous healer for our chakras, and the subsequent healing of our internal organs and systems. Chapter V looks briefly at a process to balance the chakras with your hands.

Geometry of the Aura

Our knowledge and wisdom in all areas of life are increasing rapidly as a result of the incoming energy we mentioned in Chapter I. Especially in the field of holistic health, almost daily we are discovering new and powerful techniques that heal the body and the mind.

One relatively new approach employs the geometric shapes that exist in our energy field at the etheric level. This modality of healing is based on the principles of Chiron, or *Chironic Healing*. These methods, techniques, and philosophy work so well for me that Chapter V of this book is devoted solely to an introduction to Chironic Healing.

The general philosophy and basis for Chironic Healing is that we do indeed possess a perfect pattern that can provide us health, balance, energy, and clarity of mind. This pattern exists in our energy field at the etheric level. Through our Western lifestyles and our karmic lessons, our pattern gets grossly disfigured and out of alignment, resulting in disease, illness, and pain.

This pattern can be realigned by directing and balancing the energy through lines, triangles, and diamonds that reside at the upper etheric levels (see p. 175). This particular approach originated in Australia and is now being taught around the world by Dr. Trevor Creed, who inaugurated Chironic Healing. His address and website in Australia can be found in Appendix II.

Our energy field is indeed a potpourri of energy patterns, from the Chinese meridians and the chakras system to the geometric shapes of Chironic healing. It is affected tremendously by our thoughts and emotions, and changes from moment to moment as our attention and consciousness changes. It is not necessary to know all of the intricacies of the aura, but it is good to be aware that they exist. Our *intention* and capacity to love are the keys in healing. When we heal, the Higher Intelligence will assist us in working out the details if we ask. The entire universe is structured on geometric shapes and our individual energy field is a partial reflection of these structures. *As above, so below.*

Multidimensional Self

Most of what we have covered so far in this chapter concerning our personal energy is relatively common information for the healing and health field community, and is readily available at local bookstores. However, when we look at our total energy field, our total identity, we find that there are additional dimensions upon which we exist. This arena is not as popular in the health field as most of those previously mentioned, but our whole self, our total consciousness, must be evaluated when we are attempting to achieve long-lasting health and happiness.

Dreams, for example, reveal much to us and can provide tremendous healing in our lives. Many dreams unravel our suppressed or unresolved emotions from our daily life. This type of dream usually reveals our issues in symbolic form. For example, if a man shoots you in a dream, often the shooting is a sign of an argument that has taken place or one that is coming up in your life. It rarely has anything to do with guns or actual shooting. Many of these types of dreams help us to understand and release built-up emotional stress by expressing these emotions of our life while we sleep.

Other dreams give you warning and are precognitive. This type of dream provides specific details of events that are going to occur, sometimes symbolically, sometimes literally. They are provided for your warning and may give you good information concerning your health. For example, if you dream that your vehicle is running out of gas, it could be a warning that your body is tired and running out of energy.

Dreams occur primarily, but not always, on the *astral* plane. This is a separate reality or dimension where we possess an *astral body*. Entities who leave their physical body at death, but are still attached to the Earth plane, remain primarily on the astral plane. This astral plane is as real as the physical plane we live in, and there are many levels or grades within this dimension. Some are much more refined than others. This is why sometimes upon waking our dreams seem so real to us—they are! Individuals who are excessively tired, or those with serious addictions, often find themselves feeling exhausted upon waking in the morning because they have leaked out energy on this astral plane. Their defenses are very low, and there's always something or someone ready to take their energy.

Dreams may also occur on higher, *causal* levels. This higher level of consciousness provides us with many insights, and sometimes we can receive creative thoughts and even inventions during this process. We've all heard fabulous stories of great ideas "coming to me through a dream." In this process, we are able to recall our connections to our Soul level and what is referred to as the *causal plane*. In theory, all of the archetypal forms reside on this plane. An infinite number of ideas can be received from this inner dimension of life.

The dreaming process is proof to all of us that there indeed exist other nonphysical levels of our being. We discussed how the Soul essence expresses through our physical, emotional, and mental bodies. What is not common knowledge is that the Soul is capable of expressing on many other dimensions, i.e., astral, higher mental, causal, etc., through processes such as dreaming and meditation.

As healers, it is important to be aware of these other levels on which we exist and function. Just because we don't see or feel a particular energy in a person doesn't meant that there isn't an unresolved issue or blockage lying outside of our sensory range. I personally have had many friends and clients casually drift off into a discussion of their dreams during a therapeutic session. *All of these experiences are part of the healing process—there is truly nothing that is **not** a part of this healing process.*

This is quite a general statement, but holds a powerful message for us. The point is that *we are all on a path back to conscious perfection, to Source, or God.* The beauty is that we will all get there. This is the reason why so many spiritual teachers have told us that "All is perfect," or, "The universe is perfect," or, "You are in the perfect place always." When we are conscious of this path, we accelerate our growth tremendously. *When we seek healing, or become healers in any modality, we also accelerate greatly the process of becoming whole.*

> *All of our actions and thoughts about ourselves with positive intentions are part of the healing process. Everything we say or do as a process concerning ourselves accelerates our state of wholeness, while expanding our consciousness. Proper intention is the key.*

Before leaving the subject of dreams, there is a personal experience I would like to share, because it now appears to have had many meanings, both generally and personally. It goes as follows:

> I was in the backyard of a small home in a very peaceful neighborhood. There were many children playing in the yard. It was a spring-like day—the grass was vividly green, and the fence was lined with colorful tulips on three sides of the yard. I remember that I was standing and facing toward the west.
>
> Suddenly behind me to the east was a bright, intense flash of light. It was so intense that when I awoke just moments later my head and face were actually hot! During the dream the tulips instantly started dying, one by one bending over toward the ground. I remember worrying at that point about the children. A very angelic, soft voice in the dream came from nowhere and said, "The children will all be all right."
>
> As I got ready for work the next day, I couldn't help but think of the dream and how vivid it was in my mind. I turned on the radio, and to my dismay, the news flash stated that "there had been a large explosion at the Federal Building in Oklahoma City. Many people were killed, including many children." (This building was east of where I was living at the time.)

Needless to say I was shocked. This dream took on many proportions, both as a precognitive dream and a symbolic dream. Precognitive in the event of the explosion, and symbolic in the sense of the flowers dying, but the children being protected (spiritually). I still don't quite understand how or why my face and head got so warm from the dream. The dream may have also reminded me that we sometimes travel in our dream state upon these *nonphysical* highways. The sum total of this experience validated once again for me that we do exist as multi-dimensional entities.

Another level of existence that is part of our *multidimensionality* is the causal level. This is a plane, or dimension, of pure thought and pure forms, such as archetypes. We have the ability to tap into this level, but usually it only happens through meditation or in a light, semidream state.

Great musicians and artists often tap this level and bring creative qualities and forms to our dimension. The causal level could be viewed as the pure archetype and is the home for the perfect form toward which all other forms are evolving. Causal forms originate from the highest levels of consciousness. Beyond the causal level are levels that have no forms or shapes as we know them.

Meditation is a self-controlled process that can also reveal to us our multidimensionality. It is not at all uncommon for those who have practiced for a length of time to experience sensations such as seeing color, hearing sounds, receiving verbal guidance, experiencing bliss, consciously traveling to other dimensions and making contact with other entities, receiving healing, etc. The main difference between meditation and dreaming is that we are much more in control during meditation. We have a better opportunity to remain aware of our total identity and our physical existence during the process. The experience we have in meditation is dependent upon our intention and practice.

Meditation can also be used extensively for healing, both for ourselves and others, as we shall see in the next chapter. It is a fantastic tool in helping us integrate all of our faculties and *bodies*, if you will. It's also very useful in sending a focused thought to the body, such as an affirmation or a visualization.

When one looks at the dream state and meditative experiences that are available, coupled with the overlapping of our past lives, it becomes clear that we all are multidimensional.

However, it's impossible to maintain a sense of conscious awareness at all of these levels simultaneously. *The key for healers is to be aware of these potential levels.* Many mental and emotional disorders are the result of the individual's inability to integrate all of the levels at the personality level.

Often a health problem is the result of this inability to integrate and balance our *total* being. One solution is finding a personal technique that *grounds* us. This is another benefit of meditation. The technique discussed at the end of Chapter I is excellent for grounding, and other methods will be discussed in Chapter III. When we are grounded, unwanted and unnecessary energy will flow back to Earth, helping to keep our energy field clear and balanced.

Individuals who are weak or extremely exhausted can unconsciously allow certain negative energies to enter their field. This happens frequently with alcoholics and drug abusers. We've all heard people say, "He has one drink and becomes a whole different person." This is literally true. Negative energies can also attach to someone who does not have a substance abuse problem, because negative thoughts attract negative energy. It's the law of attraction at work.

This type of possession, or attached entity, is very difficult to process, or release, without the full cooperation of the client at deeper levels of his or her being. The weakness of the client is what attracted the other entity, or negative energy, to them in the first place. Remember that only the individual soul is the real healer. As healers we must always be aware of these multidimensional energies—they can be positive or negative. For this reason alone, one must always protect the client and him- or herself with the *Light of Protection* prior to working.

The healing, or permanent releasing, of powerful negative energy will happen only when the individual is ready, and only when their vibrations and purity have reached a level where a negative energy has nowhere to attach. Then there is no longer a hook to cling to. This is a big reason why self-healing works so well.

We tend to look at purifying ourselves mostly as a physical process, like dieting or exercising, but, as we mentioned earlier, the physical level is only a portion of our identity—of our total existence—and in most cases is a reflection of our mental and emotional state. Purity and balance of mind, body, and emotions is required for us to manifest perfect health. Remember that the law of attraction is always at work, and therefore we cannot attract negativity, poor health, scattered thoughts, etc., to us when we are purified and clear—it simply cannot happen.

> *When we purify and lift our vibrations, healing is greatly accelerated. There is no place for a negative thought or emotion to attach, and blockages are released proportionate to the work that we do on ourselves.*

Our multidimensional energy field could be compared to the various layers of an onion. Old, buried issues rise to the surface as others are being released until, at last, all of our past karma and impurities are resolved. We then stand in the *light of the Soul*, masters of our life.

Mirroring Ourselves

As a society, we often tend to be extremely critical of others. This is very damaging to our health, and hinders our overall spiritual growth. Cynicism and sarcasm are like poisons to our system. They should be avoided and transcended at all costs, because these mental toxins go unseen until it is usually too late.

> *When we look at the world around us, we see our personality reflected to us as a perfect mirror.*
>
> ♦
>
> *True honesty with oneself takes courage, trust, and total love.*

How did we arrive at a state of evolution in which there are brilliant scientific discoveries daily, we can send craft to the far reaches of the solar system, have all of the conveniences imaginable, yet continually find something to complain about? What we usually fail to recognize is that another process has been established in our dimension. The world reflects back to us all of our issues, whether positive or negative.

When we see a flaw or a negative trait in another being, *it is a reflection of us, either past or present.* When we see an act of compassion or genius in another, *we are seeing ourselves do the same, or the potential for that act.* When someone is constantly making sarcastic remarks about another, they are very unhappy with themselves, yet not willing to take the necessary steps to move beyond their own limitations. *Sarcasm is a poison in our system.* To move beyond these limitations requires work and self-honesty. This is a very difficult step for most people.

We build up so many defense mechanisms and shields to protect us from harm, both real and perceived, that it takes much conscious effort to break them down and discover who we really are. This is what spiritual growth is all about: breaking through these *veils* in order to experience our real essence.

The mirroring process is important to understand because as healers it can provide much insight into a person's state and the causative factors behind the condition. When a person constantly complains about someone else, it is usually due to a karmic pattern and/or lesson that's unresolved, or simply that he or she is unconsciously projecting unwanted fragments of themselves onto this other person. When we are not happy and loving of ourselves, we tend to find things wrong with everyone else—it's so much easier than looking at ourselves!

♦ ♦ ♦

Our material world is alluring, yet often drains our energy. Television, newspapers, and all sorts of the entertainment factions are competing for our attention, our energy. Most of the advertising can seem like tentacles that reach out and grab a little bit of our energy. We must always be on the alert for such energy drains.

Here in our Western culture, we have developed into a society that constantly seeks outside fulfillment. We have movies, restaurants, races, gambling casinos, MTV, the internet, etc., We have created every form of entertainment imaginable. That's not to say in any way that having fun is bad, but we can never be integrated and whole when we are constantly chasing happiness outside of ourselves. It's a simple matter of balance.

Many people are in constant pursuit of a dream house, a dream dinner, a dream date, winning the lottery, etc. Happiness is within oneself, and nowhere else. When one is happy, *all* of life is a joy. There is no running here and there for false gratification and temporary relief of pain and unhappiness. Life is fulfilling, regardless of one's financial or social status.

We must all take stock of where we put our energy daily. How much time do you spend watching TV? Is there balance with your work life and your recreational life? *The key is balance.* This is one of our major themes as we move to the next chapter on healing yourself, but first, let's examine the overall process of integrating all that we've discussed.

What we've covered in terms of our identity is really just a small portion of who we are. In the greatest sense we are a *flame,* an extension of God. We are on the path of return to this *God awareness,* and in the process we have become fragmented, and found ourselves in a material world that is both a classroom for our growth and a dimension of infinite challenges. The flame at times *appears* nearly extinguished, and we often feel both separated from Spirit and divided within our own being.

> *The Soul is all-knowing.*
>
> ◆
>
> *Intellectual knowledge of the healing techniques or of the human energy field is not nearly as important as opening the door to the Soul energy, to love.*

But there is a light! Our Soul has never left us. It has guided us through eons of time, without failure. It is aligned with God, or Source, and has walked by our side always, never wavering or flickering for a moment. Our own Soul, or High Self, has agreed to enter this world for reasons we often do not understand. Yet, upon review, each of us will realize the great strength and character that can evolve from this *earthly* experience.

Our identity and personal energy field has many dimensions, and we possess multitudes of vibrations and energies around and within us. Do not let this confuse you. *Intellectual understanding of all of the levels is not always important to heal or to be healed! As healers, the intellectual knowledge provides us with a focus, nothing more. Healing energy comes through the heart, not the head, originating from a great Source. Our minds can help direct this energy, but the energy itself transcends intellectualism.*

It is love that is the basis for all healing—unconditional love for yourself and for others. Love opens the door for the Soul to march in and do its work. *The Soul is love and is all-knowing.* It brings forth love to the components of body, mind, and emotion. It sends love outward to the Universe.

Through the Soul all things are made whole again. The Soul is aligned with pure Spirit and can bring any type of healing energy required once the doors of love and purity are opened.

The healing energy of the Soul integrates and balances the various fragmented parts of ourselves. We are incredibly complex, yet incredibly simple from the soul level. When we open the door to our Soul energy, our life and personality becomes like a symphony. When we act and respond to the prompting of our Soul, our life becomes one of harmony, peace, and fulfillment, and our life becomes a *symphony of the Soul*.

Soul Meditation

Many meditation techniques and methods address the themes of manifestation and contact with our Soul, or High Self. Below is only one approach and it is designed from a healer's standpoint. Keep in mind that from the spiritual growth vantage point, rather than separating our Soul from our body, we wish to merge the Soul with the body. Also, when we visualize the Soul being over our head, yes there is a focal point of energy there, but the Soul is not fixed in a physical location as would be an arm or a leg.

Protection

In all environments in which we open ourselves to nonphysical energies and relax our minds and bodies, protecting ourselves is essential. There are many *energies* around us that either consciously or unconsciously are ready to merge with our energy field. Not all of these energies are desirable, nor for our highest good. Therefore always use a form of protection with which you feel good. The following is only one example of one of these procedures. The protection, like nearly every other process, is based on intention. With just a little practice, it can be accomplished in just a few seconds prior to your work.

Soul Protection Meditation

Call forth to your Soul and I Am Presence to bring forth pure light and energy for your highest good. Ask that your spiritual guides come forth and assist/protect you during this quiet time. Close your eyes and visualize the room/area you are in filled with radiant, pure white light. Seal off each wall, the floor and the ceiling with a wall of light. Know that you are protected from any unwanted energy. You may choose to light a candle, which also assists in purifying the atmosphere, play some soft, uplifting music, or light some incense. It's important that each one finds his or her protective "ritual"—one that feels right.

(As in the previous meditations, be certain to get yourself grounded to Earth. Use the meditation in Chapter I for grounding and relaxation.)

Bring your attention to the center of your chest area and feel the energy there. Begin to visualize a small white rosebud opening in this area. Sense the purity and deeper essence of this beautiful creation. Allow the flower to blossom and completely open up, sending its fragrance and essence to your entire body. Hold that feeling for a few moments. Contemplate for a moment the true essence of the white rose. Allow your mind to ponder this essence.

Now bring your awareness to a point of light about twelve inches or so above your head. Be certain your body is relaxed. Allow your breathing to be easy and rhythmic. See this point above your head as a bright sphere of radiant white light, now approximately six inches in diameter. This is your Soul focus.

Visualize a thin strand of this radiant white light descend downward from the Soul focus and enter the top of your head. As it enters it fills each and every cell in the top of the head with light energy—this energy revitalizes each cell it touches all the way to the atomic level, affecting positively your DNA structure. It rejuvenates and heals each and every particle that it penetrates. The white light contains all colors, all qualities. It can heal, transmute, energize, or provide whatever is needed in your life. Remember that your Soul knows exactly what is needed at any given time. It is important to keep open mentally to all of these positive intentions.

It is also important to feel this warm, healing energy as you see it descending. Feel it in your heart center and feeling center in the solar plexus area. Your focus at this point is for the healing and rejuvenation of your body.

Now allow it to descend slowly through the entire head area, the neck and shoulders, down the arms and the hands. See and feel it descend through the chest and upper back area, then to the lower back and abdomen. Hold it here just for a few moments and ask that it focus and heal all of your internal organs.

Continue through the genitals, hips, upper leg, knee, lower legs, and out through the feet to the ground. See yourself as a conduit for this white light healing energy to flow through. Allow this energy to flow for at least two minutes, knowing that deep, cellular healing is taking place.

As a second step, bring your attention back to the Soul focus overhead. Instead of white light descending, visualize and feel a stream of purple energy flowing down. Purple is an excellent focus for the healing of the emotional body, as well as for integrating our multidimensional selves.

As with the white light, allow the energy to slowly descend throughout the entire body. The difference with the purple energy is that you must allow it to extend outside of the body to a radius of approximately two to three feet in all directions.

Bring the purple down slowly, through the head, neck, torso, hips, legs, and feet. Now hold the energy and see and feel your entire being, mental, physical, and emotional merged in the purple. Feel the soothing effect. Know that all of your fragmented parts are being balanced and integrated. Hold this energy for at least one solid minute after you have brought it through the entire body.

This approach can be used for any color that you like, or want to receive healing from. Green is also excellent for any type of healing—it is the natural healing color for the planet. Remember that it's your intention that draws in the healing qualities and essences, not necessarily your ability to visualize. With practice this technique will become quite easy.

I am the light of the Soul, manifesting wisdom.
I am the love of the Soul, manifesting compassion.
I am whole and balanced on all levels of my being.
I am love. I am light. I am spirit manifest.

III

Principles in Self-Healing

It is no secret that there has been an enormous upsurge recently of interest in self-improvement programs and modalities. This expansion into the self-awareness areas has included many avenues, including hypnotism, meditation and yoga, color therapy, autosuggestion, biofeedback, and many others. The list is nearly infinite. This renewed interest in health and self-improvement has launched a variety of schools of thought, techniques, and methodologies. Some of these techniques have actually been around for thousands of years, while others are quite new. In the following pages we'll look at some of these methodologies, as well as provide some new insights in the field of self-healing from a spiritual and mental standpoint. No matter what you may intellectually know and understand, or what type of formal training you may have, above all else, the following is critical: *Love is the basis for all healing.*

Many of our ailments stem from a wrong or limited perspective of ourselves. Love can transmute this limitation, opening the doors to the infinite power of the Creator, and allowing it to enter your consciousness, renewing your body, mind, and Spirit.

The First Step: Loving Yourself

Learning how to love yourself is a prerequisite in the field of self-healing. Loving oneself is not always as easy as it sounds, but it truly is the shortcut to self-healing and our overall well-being. Real *self-love* is quite rare in our modern culture—a culture that emphasizes the outer appearance, the individual ego, and external success. Self-love can only manifest when the ego is quiet and one's focus lies in the depths of the heart, not on material success or ego gratification.

Loving oneself is a magical process that not only transmutes our human impurities, it also provides forgiveness unconditionally. The byproducts of real love are total forgiveness, grace, and the complete transformation of the personality matrix.

Anyone can heal himself or herself, provided they follow a few simple guidelines. The first one is faith.

> *Success in self-healing depends on the elements of faith, intention, and the belief in and acceptance of a superior power or intelligence.*

"If ye had faith, ye could move mountains." With this statement by the great teacher, Christ Jesus, lies the strength and conviction necessary to draw on the faith we all possess deep within our being. We can move the mountains and valleys within our consciousness that prevent us from reaching our goal. Faith is our power. It is our strength and provides us the ability to persevere through life's challenges. Faith gives us a belief in those things unseen or not yet experienced. There are an infinite number of examples of people throughout history who, with much less ability than many of us, have been able to overcome the most dire, dismal, or hopeless of situations and turn them into successes and growth experiences. Faith was the fuel that kept these souls going. The element of faith resides deep within our hearts.

Another element is *intention,* which provides us both the motivation and the focus we need. For people to truly want to heal themselves, they must be strongly motivated. This is a process that you can't learn in any school—there's no one saying, "OK, by such and such time, you'll have to learn this self-healing technique," or "There will be a test on Tuesday to see if you have disciplined yourself to visualize properly." This entire field of self-help requires desire and self-motivation. The old adage, "God helps those who help themselves," applies in any self-help work, especially in the field of self-healing. As we seek inner healing and expansion, the greater doors of consciousness begin to open magically. It is as if we are opening a door that has been eternally closed, and as we pull it open, there is a force on the other side pushing it toward us. It is a cocreative process.

As in all of our activities, the quality of our intention influences tremendously the desired outcome. We qualify all of our energy with the following: our individual mindset, the type of expression in our feeling nature, and our spiritual demeanor or consciousness. Does this combination sound familiar? It should. These are our primary personality expressions that we've been discussing. When considering the quality of what we are putting out to the world (or putting in our own personal, internal world), we must not only examine our personality matrix, but our moment to moment moods, our environment, our stress level. Our quality is heightened if our intentions are based in a consciousness of love and service. Our strength and energy will supersede all of our personal limitations with a consciousness of love and service.

With practice we can learn various techniques that *focus* our intentions. When we have good intentions, we are empowered many times with the spiritual forces that are always ready to assist us in our growth. We are greatly empowered by the Universe, regardless if our intentions are for ourselves or for others.

Other factors affect the quality and focus in healing, but our *intention* is the main one.

> *There is only one energy in the Universe—our intention gives this energy the primary quality and focus that is required for all forms of healing.*

Thirdly, our *belief and acceptance in a Higher Power* opens us to a superior healing energy and intelligence, which provides us with the healing power that we need. This occurs at whatever level and in whatever degree we need it. We may not consciously know the exact cause of a problem, nor the specifics on how to heal our body, but *our Higher Self knows. The Supreme Intelligence knows.* When we call for this Higher Source to help and assist us, we open up to grand levels and infinite possibilities. This belief and openness is a byproduct of our original faith. As in all areas of our life, our belief system grows and strengthens, and our confidence builds with practice and experience.

Without this belief in a Higher Power, we limit ourselves in all aspects of our life, including our ability to heal ourselves. With the openness to this power we become unlimited. To employ this Higher Power and energy, we simply need to ask for it. Statements such as, "I call forth to my High Self to heal me," or, "I call forth my own I AM Presence and the Beings of Light to assist me in healing," work wonderfully. Spiritual beings on many levels are here to help us—they only need to be called! It's like having an electrical outlet in your home for your computer—the power is there, all you need to do is just plug it in!

In Chapter I, we mentioned the process of learning our life's lessons and how these lessons are many times translated into physical ailments and limitations of infinite variety. Not all of our afflictions or imperfections are a reflection of a major lesson to be learned or processed in our life, but all of our physical limitations do reflect a blockage of some type in our personal energy field. This blockage can be mental, emotional, or physical (the etheric*).

When we experience pain or discomfort in any way, it is an indication that our Soul, our real self, is not completely expressing itself. Pain is like the oil light in our car—when it comes on we need to pull over immediately and check our oil before it's too late. Pain is the signal, just like the oil light, that something is wrong with our system. It points to the area of blockage that we need to address.

When we are in a healthy condition, our Soul energy is able to express through us and we are whole, fulfilled, and balanced. We are in alignment with this higher aspect of ourselves. We could say our personal symphony is being performed.

> *Health may be defined as: "A state in which we harmoniously and clearly are expressing ourselves at all levels— physically, emotionally, and mentally."*

---

* In the older, more traditional mystical studies, the etheric level (discussed in Chapter II) was considered to be part of the same vehicle as the physical. In this school of thought, the physical plane or dimension is one and the same as the etheric; only a slight difference in vibration exists. Most clairvoyants and sensitives, especially in the healing field, can see and feel this etheric *body*, or template.

Achieving a Balanced Life

To achieve happiness and health at any level, we must have balance in our lives. Balance has been a central theme in my personal path, and appears to be a general process that everyone is addressing either consciously or otherwise. To be healthy and happy we need to be balanced. It's that simple. We need to work, play, share, rest, exercise, socialize, be quiet, create, etc. Being the unique individuals that we are, all of our personal balance sheets in this regard are going to be quite different. What balanced living means to one may not apply at all for another.

For example, a professional athlete will naturally expend much more energy physically than perhaps an engineer or doctor would. A research scientist will expend much more mental energy than say an athlete. These examples are obviously quite general, but each one of these groups and individuals must nevertheless be expressing on all three of the major levels to maintain a balanced life.

If a weightlifter spends all his time working out, with all of his focus on building the body, his Soul is deprived of mental and emotional expression. If an engineer spends all of her energy on developing a new type of telephone communication system, she is depriving herself of physical and emotional expression, not to mention the possible lack of social interface. You get the point.

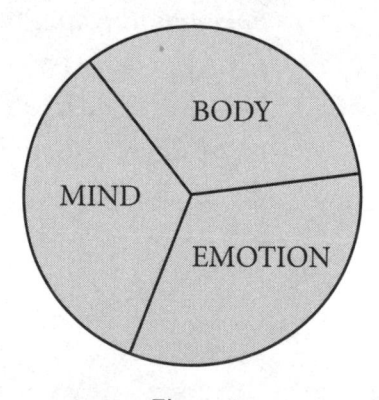

Figure 1
Balancing Mind, Body,
and Emotions

Figure 1 is a very basic pie graph that shows three major areas of personality expression.

I struggled somewhat in using this type of chart because it may be perceived as *too* analytical. There is also much overlap of each section into the other that the graph doesn't reveal. I call it "My Little Pie Graph of Life."

This is a great starting tool for personal balance. As a test, draw a circle like this one. In each area list your activities and involvements that help you express, either physically, mentally, or emotionally. Do you feel balanced in your life? In what areas do you feel lack or blockage? How can you balance your graph—more exercise, more recreation, more study time, better, clearer emotional expression? Are you expressing openly in all three areas? What is balance for you?

There are an infinite number of ways to express who we are, ourselves, or our energy. Figure 2 is another example of this. It's a handy tool to perform the same exercise with this chart. Am I spending too much time at work? Do I have a fulfilling social life (recreation)? Do I spend enough time being quiet and getting focused? Remember that this is what balance si for you. We are all very unique, and what is the proper time for recreation or rest for one is not necessarily the same amount for someone else. Watching a movie may be an excellent recreation for one person, but boring for someone more socially oriented. A light jog or walk in the woods may be a good workout for one, while an hour of exercise at the local health spa is a good workout for another.

Figure 2
Balancing Our Energy

Balance is critical in all aspects of our life, whether we're creating artistically, spending time in a close relationship, managing a large number of people, or just simply leading a very busy life. Our culture could learn a lot from the Chinese attitude on balance. They view life as a dynamic, everchanging yin and yang energy that continually shifts and moves—and then seeks balance again. In our personal life this translates primarily to active/passive, masculine/feminine, action/rest, structure/creativity, etc. Considering that our biorhythms and energy levels move in cycles, look closely at these polarities in your daily life. If you are a very active person, do you allow yourself time to reflect and relax? Whether you are a male or a female, are you able to express traditionally masculine qualities (assertiveness, adventurousness, physical energy, etc.) in balance with the feminine qualities (intuition, sensitivity, understanding, nurturing, etc.)?

From the spiritual growth standpoint, we are all on a path to wholeness and completeness within ourselves. That includes perfect balance in the masculine and feminine, whether you are male or female. For example, many women need to be more assertive, while many men need to become more sensitive. Only when we have achieved this male/female balance will we reach fulfillment and happiness, because we no longer seek this balance, or depend on it outside of ourselves.

Our Soul expresses through the three *bodies* we discussed in Chapter II. When it comes to balancing our life as conscious spiritual beings, our spiritual nourishment becomes part of the equation. In essence, our Soul is always seeking expression through each of us. Some are simply more aware of their spiritual longings and prompting than others. We are all at different, unique rungs of the spiritual ladder.

Figure 3 adds this spiritual, or Soul expression aspect to our little pie graph. When we are balanced and integrated, the expressions of this pie graph will merge into one unified energy field that is clearly expressing our highest potentials.

Figure 4 is another presentation of this fourfold energy. The Soul is represented at the center, since in reality it is our *center* behind the personality.

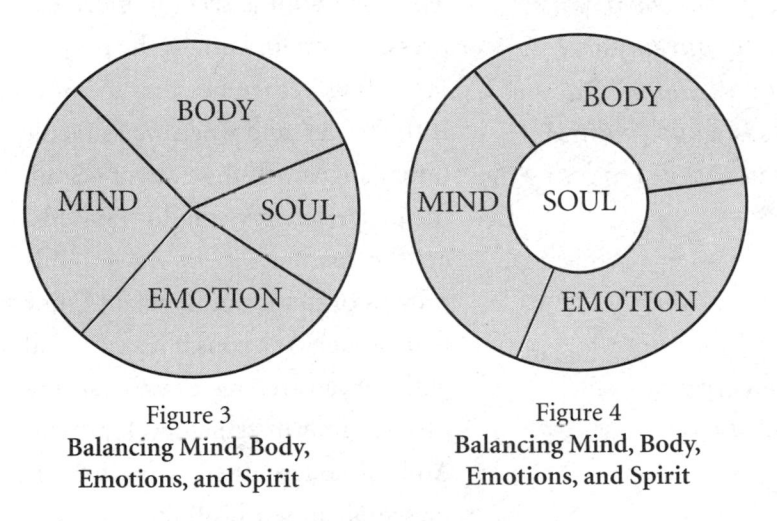

Figure 3
Balancing Mind, Body,
Emotions, and Spirit

Figure 4
Balancing Mind, Body,
Emotions, and Spirit

Behind all of our actions is the energy of the Soul, attempting to express clearly and completely our true nature. Some individuals are on the conscious path of manifesting this energy, utilizing their highest potentials. Those who are not on this conscious path, who are basically not seeking any spiritual fulfillment, nevertheless are entrusted with some measure of spiritual energy. For example, we all know individuals who are extremely compassionate, or who are doing tremendous community service, or possibly someone in the arts who doesn't necessarily consider themselves to be on a spiritual path. In these cases it's easy to see that, whether they accept it or not, they are manifesting a certain quota of their soul energy in their daily life. It may not be clear, and it may not always be of the highest intention, but there is spiritual energy being expressed just the same.

Why is this understanding important in healing? When someone is ill, especially with a chronic problem, their soul is seeking more expression and growth. In the process of healing, remember that the Soul is the healer, and when we as facilitators align with the patient's Soul, the proper energy will flow. Whether the patient is aware of this process or not is unimportant. They will awaken to a conscious spiritual path or awareness exactly at the proper time in their development. And, of course, these same principles apply in self-healing.

Self-healing can only take place when we begin to know and understand ourselves. "Man, know thyself," the age-old adage for the spiritual warrior, applies no where better than in the arena of self-healing. Self-healing begins with self-evaluation and self-honesty. Honesty with ourselves is only possible when we have begun to totally accept ourselves.

Looking at the above charts and examples, can you be honest in evaluating your life? Can you be courageous enough to admit your imbalances? Are you determined enough to change and set the proper intentions in motion to balance your life? Are you aware that thousands of souls before you have conquered

> *The degree of clarity and balance of our physical, emotional, and mental aspects is what qualifies our Soul expression.*
>
> ♦
>
> *Total acceptance of ourselves is one of the highest expressions of true self-love.*

life on our plane of existence and become masters of their own being?

Our personal path indeed represents a symphony. We move through our daily lives with our physical, emotional, mental, and spiritual instruments, and like a symphonic orchestra, if only one small instrument is out of key, the entire orchestra is affected.

Visualization

Before going to the next phase of specific self-healing methods, I would like to share with you a powerful and long-lasting experience I had a few years ago with self-healing. This experience validated my beliefs in self-healing and strengthened my convictions in the field of mental power and visualization.

About fifteen years ago I had begun to experience much pain and stiffness in my neck area. I had begun chiropractic treatment (adjustments), and had the usual X-rays. The diagnosis was that I had severe disc (the soft tissue between the vertebrae) damage in the neck area between C5 and C6 (Cervical vertebraes 5 and 6). The doctor at that time, along with at least three others over the next ten years, all stated the same thing: that in my youth I must have suffered a severe fall or collision of some type to have such deterioration occur. The only incident I could remember that would possibly cause any damage was during high school football season. No one incident came to mind until much later, during a meditation session.

The adjustments helped, but the relief did not last very long. I also was guided to acupuncture as a treatment and it helped as well. Eventually, I also received massage therapy, and again there was relief. However, the relief I received was always temporary—maybe for a couple of days or a week at best. There were times when the pain was so severe that I would awake in the middle of the night and couldn't roll over without using my hands to turn my head. My frustration mounted, since I wanted to become more of a healer myself. "How could I be a good example of a healer when I had such a chronic ailment?" I would ask myself.

I started looking for any help in understanding the problem I could get. A big help was Louise Hay's book *You Can Heal Your Life.* She states that neck problems often stem from inflexibility. That made me realize that possibly I was holding some very rigid thoughts and attitudes. Was I being too inflexible with my children? Too inflexible with my subordinates at work? More importantly, was I too inflexible with my perceptions of what a *spiritual path* was all about? This exercise helped a great deal—relieving much of the underlying cause of the problem. By reexamining my perceptions and attitudes, other, more fixed areas of my life began to come into balance.

Finally I sought spiritual help and guidance. I consulted a very spiritual and intuitive friend in Arizona and was given strong advice that I indeed had the power within myself to heal my own neck and spinal area. I was told that I was truly on the right path, but needed a little more perseverance and faith in my approach to self-healing. I was very inspired to think and know that I was going to heal myself and get relief! I could already feel the healing start! I was now thoroughly motivated. Something inside clicked. I knew this would work!

Here were my specific guidelines and suggestions: take twenty minutes a day for about two weeks for each vertebra. Visualize each one being perfect in structure and integrity. I also visualized the soft tissue (cartilage and muscle) around each area to be perfect and whole as well.

I instantly pulled out my *Gray's Anatomy* and began studying the structure and outline of each vertebrae (specifically, the cervical bones in the neck), as I had not yet taken an anatomy course. I followed my friend's instructions to the *max*. Each night before falling asleep I would go into a meditation and focus on one of the vertebrae in my neck, starting at the top, or C1 (Cervical Vertebrae 1). I spent two weeks on each one in the neck, twenty minutes each at a minimum. Twenty minutes seemed like a long time at first, but later the session became quite natural. It was somewhat easier for me than perhaps others because of my years of meditation exercises and mental disciplines.

After only two days of this visualization, I began to feel much relief in my neck. I could turn it without pain. It became more flexible. I was sleeping all night. By practicing this before falling asleep I was setting up a pattern in my subconscious that continued the healing process while sleeping. I was feeling very positive about this process, and my confidence was building. *The positive, joyful feelings were also fueling my visualizations, and energizing the healing process.*

The key was my intention and faith, but it was strengthened by my focus to the specific area, along with my positive feelings. I would hold my hands on the vertebrae I was healing, and visualize only the perfect vertebrae, while surrounding and bathing the area in pure white light. It worked! Rarely do I get stiff necks anymore, and when they do manifest, they are very minor. I do not have any pain in the neck area. My nights are very restful.

Two tremendous insights resulted from this experience. First, I realized that if I could do this, almost anyone who applied himself or herself could also heal themselves. Second, if I had the innate ability to facilitate the healing in my neck, I could use this same process to heal any other ailment that may arise in my body. I later found this to be true.

A byproduct of this kind of visualization is that it will manifest in your life a practitioner or modality that is suited for you and your ailment and provide any additional support necessary, or it may bring to you a new diet, a new book on self-improvement, or any number of infinitely possible tools that will facilitate the healing of your specific problem.

When you visualize your own health, you begin the healing process within, as well as drawing to you any additional external support necessary.

It's the *law of attraction* at work again. Do not limit yourself as to the best method that will heal you. The Universe is infinite and can fulfill your thought form, your desire to be healed, in many creative ways. The only limitation is your thoughts and beliefs. Remember the basic guidelines: *intention, faith, and the belief in a Higher Power.*

During this period of my visualization exercises, covering many months, I was also drawn intuitively to a new chiropractor in my area. I kept noticing over and over again his picture in the local paper, then realized that I must see him. He practiced the BEST method (Bio-Energetic Synchronization Technique), and his adjustments were very light and not forceful. The BEST method, as discussed in Chapter II (see p. 45), utilizes your own breathing and energy centers to assist your body in realigning itself through the nervous and muscular systems.

When one visualizes a perfect or natural condition, as was the case with my neck, the Universe follows that perfect pattern—*energy follows thought.* Consequently my subconscious mind and the rest of my consciousness, including the physical and emotional, were following the thought of a perfect spinal column. Concurrently, the *perfect thought* of my neck was attracting any and all elements to facilitate and manifest that thought in the physical reality. In this case it was a new doctor who was more in alignment with my belief system at the time, and one who totally supported as well my own self-healing technique. The law of attraction will draw to you any additional elements you need for your healing, whether it's a doctor, a massage therapist, an herbalist, a counselor, a book, etc.

Before each session of visualization I would also perform a type of meditation or prayer and ask for my own High Self to assist me in healing my neck. I intuitively knew that I couldn't consciously understand or picture in my mind the precise detail of my vertebrae as well as my own High Self could, or my Soul could. Again, the Soul always knows what needs healed— and when. I called forth my spiritual guides as well to help with the details.

Additionally, I visualized myself doing my usual daily activities, but *with much flexibility and no stress or pain in the neck area.* I many times pondered, had I used the phrase, "This is a real pain in the neck," once too often? Or the more popular one, "He (or she) is a real pain in the neck"? I immediately canceled these phrases from my mind and routine!

The results were nearly instant. Within a few days, my recovery started, and over four years later, I remain flexible and pain free in the neck area. I occasionally receive preventative treatments, but rarely do I have stiff necks anymore, and when I do, I follow the same routine as above, and the results are nearly instant, in just one session. I have since used this visualization process in many other areas of my life, from my physical health to relationships to finances. The results are inevitable, and come down to one simple fact: *energy follows thought.*

Whatever we put our thought into, whether it's money, our hobbies, or our homes, there will be much energy attracted to it. This is very important to understand in all aspects of healing, whether it's self-healing or the healing of others. The only real blockage or limitation to this process is the situation in which the Soul has not agreed, due to the fact that certain lessons have not yet been learned. Even in these cases, partial healing will nearly always occur.

> *In self-healing, the perfect thought sets up the pattern for health. Add the feelings of love and joy to the thought, then use will power to send the thought form. Health will manifest— it is the law!*

We are truly the creators of our universe, and of course our universe includes our bodies and our overall condition. As the creators of our personal universe, our thoughts tend to be our design, our *blueprints* of our creation. Our emotions tend to be the fuel, or the builder, that empowers this blueprint. It is very similar to an architectural design: the architect places his plan on a blueprint. It gets reviewed and revised. Then the final plan goes to the builder, and it is manifested in the physical realm through physical energy. Our thought process parallels this process exactly. The more clear the thought, the more specific the result. The more positive and powerful the emotion, the quicker and more the complete the manifestation. This is again the law of attraction at work.

When working with the principles of self-healing, there are two parallel paths, or processes, we must look at. The first one is getting at the root cause of the problem. In the first two chapters we discussed the energy behind the physical manifestation, and the concept of how thought and emotion play a major role in the condition of our physical body. The second path is the actual self-healing that you can perform, utilizing techniques that coincide very much with my own example given above.

Cause

Choose a disease or affliction that has been bothering you or ailing you for quite some time. Pick a condition in which other practitioners have not been able to completely heal or correct, since there are probably some deeper, causative factors at work.

Spend some quiet time addressing your problem, which we will now refer to as your "imperfection." Try to always avoid using negatives in describing your, or someone else's, condition—remembering the subconscious patterns which are reinforced by your thoughts. Statements such as, "I am sick of this ache," or, "My problem won't go away," or, "I have been told for twenty years by doctors that I will always have this pain," all reinforce and energize the negative condition. Always energize the correct condition.

Because energy always follows thought, fueling negativity through constant discussion and worry will usually only make the condition worse, and consequently more difficult to correct. That's not to say that you must avoid or not address the issue or imperfection, only to energize the perfect condition. Again,

> *Give no energy to the negative, to the blockage. Give only positive energy to the desired outcome, to the perfect condition.*

there's no replacement for common sense. We do not want to commit the sin of omission, but quite the opposite. We want to uncover, explore, weed out, delete, heal, or whatever it takes to get to the root of the problem, the blockage.

Counselors, especially those with a metaphysical/spiritual base, along with dream therapy, psychology, hypnotism, and other avenues, can help in uncovering some of the causes of your imperfection. There are many good therapists available who can assist you in uncovering some of the possible causes of your affliction. However, the true, specific factors are *best known only by you, and uncovered by yourself.* Simply start examining the cause that lies underneath your physical imperfection. Ask inwardly to discover this cause. Sometimes the real cause is more obvious than you think. Remember to "Ask and ye shall receive."

When you are out of balance in some area of your life, your body will always give you a message to alert you. For example, a stiff elbow or knee may mean that you simply are not flexible in your attitudes and belief systems. If it occurs on just one arm, then maybe you are not balanced in your active/passive continuum. If your right elbow is always stiff, then maybe you are too active (or too inactive), and need more passive time or more rest. Maybe you are too aggressive or too passive in your daily life.

If you have very sensitive skin, or are thin skinned, then maybe you are too sensitive to what others think and say. If you are nearsighted, that is, you cannot see what's close to you, maybe you are overlooking some key elements in your personal life. You may have the big picture clearly in your mind, but are overlooking more obvious details that need addressed.

Meditations

These are just some simple examples to help you get started in the process. The following is a process in the form of a meditation designed to help bring the cause of your imperfection to your conscious mind. Remember that until the cause behind the imperfection is corrected, we will have continually recurring problems (imperfections, I should say!).

Meditation on Cause

Get yourself relaxed and quiet. Call forth to your Soul to provide you clear information that will reveal the cause behind any imperfection reflected in your body. Remember that your Soul knows everything about you. It is not separate from you, it only appears that way. All information about the past or present is stored at this level and can be brought forth to your consciousness. Again, "Ask and ye shall receive."

Once relaxed, mentally go to the area of your body you want to heal. Mentally talk to that area. Ask it, "What happened?" "What would you like me to do to help?" Talk to it as if it were a hurt, innocent child, somewhat separate from yourself.

Be open to all possibilities. A physical accident, a type of karmic incident, may have happened many years earlier and is not in your conscious memory. Or, possibly an emotional pattern such as resentment, hatred, or anger may have fueled or put energy in this area of your body over time and created the imperfection. There may be a locked memory, one very painful from your childhood, that will be revealed. This blockage must be processed in order for the energy to flow in this area.

It is important not to avoid emotional issues at this point. If a painful experience or memory surfaces, go through it. If you need to cry or scream, do it. The avoidance of pain is many times the avenue that prevents you from being healed. Locked-up or suppressed pain can create an emotional blockage, which is reflected eventually as a physical blockage or pain. Remembering all of the exact details is not necessary.

*Do not be discouraged if you do not get an immedi-
ate answer. It will come. It may come in the form of a
book that a friend gives you, an article in a magazine,
or overhearing another conversation at work. It may
come as an intuitive flash or insight, because we have
all answers within us. Also, you always get what you
ask for. Do this exercise every day for at least two
weeks, then let it go for a while. You will be surprised
at the information that starts coming to you, and in a
variety of forms.*

*If you do not practice meditation, it helps to per-
form this technique as you are falling asleep. You may
get insights during your dream state, or just as you are
awakening in the morning. Use your intuition, and
allow the universe to bring to your consciousness the
precise answer you are pursuing.*

Remember that imperfections are a normal part of life,
especially when viewed from the perspective that we choose
certain lessons to learn. From the spiritual level, there is no
imperfection. We should aspire always to manifest perfection
in all of our life. Total health is always possible, no matter in
what circumstance or current condition we find ourselves.

This ideal condition is more challenging when we also consider that society is continually sending us negative programming. For example, in the fall of the year we are bombarded
with cold and flu ads, which send the message to millions that
"it's time to get sick again"! When we have a headache, we're
told to take an aspirin, which only addresses the symptom, not
the problem. Or, "If you get your feet wet, you'll catch a cold."
We must always be alert to the input we are receiving, especially through television, so that we do not allow our subconscious
to set up or support a negative pattern of imperfection or

disease throughout our body. Positive affirmation is a technique that helps counter the negative programming that has been set up in our subconscious over a period of many years. We'll look more closely at this technique later in this chapter.

Going back to the concept of avoiding an issue or avoiding pain, are there activities and/or habits you have adopted in order to avoid an issue in your life? This is a key question, since people literally spend much of their lives chasing people, places, and doing all sorts of things simply to avoid their own inner condition. Drug addiction, alcoholism, codependency, sex, gambling, overeating, or any activity taken to the degree of attachment and abuse are all activities we often use simply to avoid a painful or frightening condition that is being suppressed from conscious awareness.

Obviously no one likes pain—or at least most people don't! Maybe those who do have another issue they are working out! The good news is that when a person goes through an emotional release from a past hurt, painful or not, doors of health and energy begin to open unlike anything before. Limitations vanish, and new hope and promise for a much happier life emerge. It is never too late to experience rejuvenation and a new life of health, vitality, and joy!

Self-Healing Technique

A second path to take in self-healing is the direct process of utilizing mental, healing energy through visualization and affirmation. Keep in mind we're focusing on two major parallel paths. Many other processes are still going on as well; i.e., keeping yourself in balance as discussed earlier, watching your diet, visiting a physician, possibly spending time with nature, joining a prayer or healing group, reading about the imperfection you are currently experiencing, etc. *You should be open to any*

*and all material, practitioners, methods, and possibilities sur-
rounding the correction of your condition. Place no limitation on
understanding your condition, or how that condition can be completely cured.*

As for the direct healing, learn all you can about the area
that's not perfect. If necessary, buy an anatomy book and look
up and study your body part. *Gray's Anatomy* is excellent. For
example, if you have a chronic knee imperfection, look up that
joint in the book. Study the bone structure and the soft tissue
(cartilage, tendons, ligaments, muscles, etc.) arrangement in
that area. Get a fairly good picture in your mind of what your
knee should look like anatomically. Because intention is one of
the keys in our healing process, detailed visualization is not
absolutely necessary, but it does assist greatly in our focus.

Before actually going into a visualization session, remember
to bring in your feeling nature. Our mind will send the mental
image of the perfect knee, and our heart will send the necessary *love energy* and fuel to build it. Our mind is the architect,
the designer—our heart and feeling center are the builders.

> *Our mind and our heart
> should work together in
> all forms of healing.*

Before you start your visualization, be sure that you are in a positive, dynamic state of being. Accept
yourself as you are on a deeper level,
the level where you exist as perfection. Accept your condition, do not
resist it. You may say, "This is only
temporary," or, "This imperfection is only an illusion," but
remember your condition is there for a reason—it could be
karmic, it could be a tremendous opportunity for you to learn
to heal yourself and others, or it could simply be the result of
emotional or psychological stress.

If you haven't started to do this yet, start now to truly love yourself, no matter what your state of being may be. If you are in a negative emotional state, love yourself for feeling that way. If you have moments of feeling hopeless, love yourself for feeling hopeless. Loving yourself will always uplift you, it will fuel your healing process and intention with positive energy and help

> *Loving yourself is the single most important factor in self healing. Loving yourself brings total self-acceptance, self-confidence, and self-esteem in the greatest sense.*

you release the limiting, unnecessary elements that are holding you back. Only love can open your feeling nature in positive, uplifting ways. reread the poem at the opening of this book often—it holds much value in this spirit of loving yourself.

Self-Healing Meditation

For starters, allow yourself at least twenty minutes a day for two weeks, then one or two days off. Twenty minutes twice a day is even better—morning and evening. One of the best times is just before falling asleep, because this sets up a powerful, positive pattern at the subconscious level, healing you all night and the following day.

As a protocol, before each session call forth to your High Self and spiritual guides to assist you. "I invoke my High Self and the Creator of All to assist me in healing myself. Help me in those areas and specifics in which I am not yet aware. I ask to heal and be healed in my _____ area." Visually surround the room you are in and your body in a pure, white aura of the Light of Protection.

Get relaxed through deep breathing. Allow your thoughts to slow down and your emotions to become calm. In your mind's eye, bring in the perfect body condition for the area you are going to heal. Start sending love from your heart to that area of your body. Ask that this love continue to flow throughout the meditation and afterward as well.

Focus now on the perfect body condition. If you can't stay focused, then call for your Soul or High Self to send the perfect mental image and healing there. If you can't picture the are to be healed or focus mentally, then send love and light to that area. Your High Self will focus the specifics for you. It is important to feel the love energy flowing to your body or area of life that needs healed. This positive feeling element is critical to your success.

Hold the perfect image for a minimum of twenty minutes, perhaps a little less in the beginning. Know that healing is indeed taking place. As you are holding the perfect image, see the area surrounded in pure light. If you like and are able, place one or both hands on the area. This will assist you in focusing. Feel the warmth and energy of your hands. Allow this warmth to energize your faith and sense the healing that is taking place.

Before coming out of the meditation, see yourself having fun and in a state of perfect health. See yourself doing something that you currently are restricted in doing because of your imperfection. See yourself full of joy and energy—see yourself clearly in your ideal state, and surround that perfect condition in light.

As you begin to build a focus, create an affirmation such as the one here that will set the proper thought pattern in your subconscious. (As you repeat the words, feel the thought and healing energy pour into your body.)

**I am perfect at all levels of my being,
my body is free of all blockages.
I am at peace within myself,
I am light, I am light, I am light.**

There are many methods to help you heal yourself. This meditation opens the door for one powerful method that has proven to be successful. It is a form of mental healing and requires the ability, to some extent, to use the mind for visualization. Visualization requires a certain measure of creative imagination as well as discipline. This technique parallels some popular schools of thought that suggest a person can heal themselves of various serious diseases, such as cancer, through creative visualization. There are many, many documented cases in which people have truly healed and cured themselves completely of serious and even terminal conditions using creative visualization, at least as a supplement to the healing process.

An example, and one that I have used occasionally for stress goes as follows. When I have stress in my upper back/shoulder area, I go into a meditation and visualize the stress points forming in the shape of wooden dowels. Then I visualize a large claw hammer gently coming down from overhead, slowly and gently pulling out the dowels. I see it and feel it. Each time I use this approach it amazes me just how powerful our minds really are. These types of visualization require caution, however. You must be disciplined enough to follow all of the way through the process. You can never stop in the middle, or you'll end up energizing the imperfection! Again, success is quicker when the feelings are utilized with the meditation.

Another example of visualization can be applied when the body is infected with a virus. Visualize millions of white blood cells turning into small, white soldiers. See and feel these soldiers attacking and wiping out the virus. Visualize only healthy blood cells existing in your entire body.

Look at any imperfection you may have in your body. What type of creative visualization might work to help remove this blockage? Think of something similar to the above two examples that might work, or use one of them to start with. Always invoke your own Soul and High Self, along with your spiritual guides, and be persistent. Give the technique at least twenty minutes a day for two weeks minimum before you evaluate your success.

Let's never forget the necessity for common sense and the expertise and professionalism of the current medical field. Even though the techniques and philosophies outlined in this book do indeed work, they do not supersede those situations that require immediate medical attention. Any chronic condition we find in ourselves took quite some time to manifest, and usually will take a bit of time to heal. Those that are serious and life-threatening need the attention and treatment of a trained medical professional who is experienced and trained to heal you in those situations. We should never forget the immeasurable service they have provided to humanity, and continue to provide to us now.

In a very real sense, only our own mind, our belief system, can limit us. As we open up more and more to our Higher Self, our Soul, limitations begin to fall away and we step into the realm of infinite possibilities. I remember a saying I'll never forget that I read in a church some twenty years ago: "One with God is a majority." That pretty much says it all in terms of what is possible in our life.

Affirmation

Our natural state of being is complete, fulfilled, peaceful, and joyous, but for all the reasons discussed earlier in the book, we often feel separated and fragmented in our life. One way to return to our fulfilled, complete, and integrated state is to reaffirm our wholeness and our perfection, or, in other words, reverse our trends and habits by replacing our subconscious, negative programming with positive, dynamic affirmations.

Affirmations, again with proper intention and perseverance, can virtually transform our lives. When we repeat anything long enough in our mind, it filters through to our subconscious. The subconscious mind functions twenty-four hours a day, sending the quality and power of the thoughts that we have programmed to our body. When we add to our affirmation positive, dynamic feelings and emotion, it becomes even more powerful. Remember that our emotional energy is the fuel for our thoughts.

I personally focus on mental affirmations, though verbal affirmations are powerful as well. The most powerful of all starts with *"I am,"* followed by the desired outcome, such as *"I am abundant,"* or, *"I am healed."* These are obviously very general, but preceding your affirmation with *"I am"* makes the statement more powerful. The *"I am"* actually sets up a vibration, a frequency, that rings through from the highest levels of your being to the densest.

Remember on the mountain when Moses was ready to return with the Ten Commandments what God told Moses when he ask God, "Who should I tell them that I am?" God responded, *"Tell them I Am that I Am."* The *"I Am"* is our true and pure identity as Spirit, as God-Self. It is the individualized pure spirit, or essence, that is a spark of God. Any time we use the *"I Am"* in an affirmation we draw energy from this spiritual level, the level of true knowing and true identity—the level of real power. *This energy and power can heal anything—it knows no limitations.*

Here are some suggestions for creating your own affirmation:

♦ Always affirm the perfect condition for the area you are healing; i.e., never include the negative state in your affirmation. For example, for an ailing ankle, do not say, "I am healing my sore ankle." A better affirmation might include, "I am manifesting a perfect ankle of light," or, "I see myself walking and running as a child, without pain and unlimited."

♦ When you have discovered a possible mental or emotional cause of a physical ailment, include in your affirmation statements that heal this cause. For example, if you have a chronic knee problem, the underlying cause may be an inflexible attitude. In your affirmation, include a corrective statement such as, "I trust life and flow easily with life's processes," or, "I am flexible and understanding to the ideas and thoughts of others." With practice, you will intuitively know just the right phrasing.

♦ Precede as many statements as possible with the "I Am."

♦ Keep the statements fairly short.

♦ There are numerous affirmations throughout the book that can give you an idea or suggestion on how to put your own together. It helps tremendously if the affirmation statements have a rhythm that you personally like. For starters, use the one on page 101, but with more specifics on your area of healing.

♦ Repeat the affirmation several times. There is no specific number—just *intuit* it.

When repeating the affirmation, always put positive, joyful feelings into the affirmation, whether you repeat them out loud or not. Also, it's most powerful if you can visualize the perfect condition while you are doing the affirmation. This takes a little practice, but accelerates the process tremendously.

Take a moment and write out an affirmation that's meant just for you—no one else need ever see it. Think of a condition that you would like to heal. Using the tools above, write out about a four- or five-line affirmation that affirms the perfect, healed condition and your overall happiness. Make it fun and exciting. Remember that your affirmation is a powerful tool that will assist you in your healing and growth process. Make this process fun and as exciting as possible—you *will* get results.

Relationships

Most of what we call personal karma is being worked out, or *balanced*, in the arena of relationships. It's clear to most of us that our emotional pain and anguish usually comes in relating to another—emotionally, that is.

We have friends that anger us, we have lovers that leave us, we have family members that take us for granted, we have bosses who overpower us—the list is endless. In reality, we either allow this condition, or many times merely perceive the process as him or her hurting us. Yes, we have our personal frustrations and challenges in our particular field of endeavor, such as sports, education, research, etc., that require attention and patience, but nearly all of the emotional pain and hurt is the result of a personal relationship of some type with another human being. These hurts and relationships can be healed also.

Before we can *heal* a relationship, we must honestly and clearly confront the issue. How many times has a personal situation manifested over and over in your life? A classic example is the employee who finds his or her boss overpowering, game-playing, extremely arrogant, or manifesting any number of negative qualities. The employee quits the job, only to find that the next boss, who is usually of the same sex as the previous one, has similar personality traits. When this experience repeats itself, we can be sure there's a major healing within us that must take place, or a lesson to be learned. Quite possibly the employee had treated many people the same way in a previous lifetime, or similarly, as their current boss does, or at least had some similar personality traits, or this could simply be a less to learn: a lesson in standing up for oneself, a lesson humility, or any number of growth opportunities.

By confronting this type of relationship with the intention to heal, we may more quickly move through any lesson that's needed and not have to go through the same type of relationship ever again. *It's not important that we know if it is a past-life karmic situation or not. What is critical is that we confront it in the present with the intention to resolve.*

Even more powerful are our personal, intimate relationships—lovers, spouses, and other family members. These relationships are more difficult at times because of the deep emotional connections. What makes this type of relationship more difficult is that many times we don't want to leave the relationship, only to improve it, and improving it means feeling better about the relationship and feeling better about ourselves. We often struggle to improve a personal relationship and in the process we continue to feel worse about it, because the relationship may no longer serve our highest good.

Before we look at a very powerful relationship meditation, here are some suggestions on working through relationships:

- ♦ The world mirrors ourselves back to us. This is especially true of those closest to us. What we see in them is nearly always a projection of ourselves, past or present. Continually finding fault in another reflects an unhappiness within yourself.

- ♦ The more intense a relationship is, the more likely it is karmic. This doesn't always mean that it is necessarily with the same person that you are balancing your past actions, but many times it is. By knowing of a karmic pattern, we can more quickly move through it by asking, "What is my lesson(s) here?"

- ♦ As long as we are reacting to any situation, rather than acting appropriately, we are not getting out of the loop—we are not growing. Constantly reacting to someone else's actions toward you takes you away from yourself. In the extreme, this is "mob consciousness." We must always step back in relationships and evaluate how we truly feel, not only about the other person, but about the relationship itself. Am I acting to my true nature, or am I reacting to the other person? Is this a relationship I want to continue and improve, or one that doesn't support my Highest Good (or my partner's) at this time? Does the relationship bring me long-term joy? We must do our very best to become the observer to the relationship when we are evaluating it. This is extremely challenging!

- ♦ Most people need to be accepted by others. (Yes, most. There are those who do not concern themselves much with this issue, but they tend to be the exception, not the rule, and are usually at one end of the polarity or the other—enlightened or extremely unenlightened.) If you're staying in a personal relationship, or simply want to keep a friend because you need to be accepted, the relationship is not complete because you are probably not secure within yourself. You may also need to reevaluate your own security so that you do not fear the loss of the friend. It may very well be a time in your relationship when you should both move on, growing in your own personal path.

On the next page are two meditations that can help greatly in challenging relationships.

Working Relationships Meditation

This type of meditation is helpful for business associates, conflicts at work, and for meetings that you may anticipate being very difficult. Get yourself quieted, focused, and know you'll be without interruption for at least twenty minutes. Ask that you be able to focus your consciousness in your High Self and that you want to communicate directly to the individual you are concerned with, but only communicate with their High Self.

See this person(s) in your mind. Talk to this person(s) directly. Say, "I honor and respect you, and I want us to have a harmonious and clear relationship." See a beam of light connecting your mind to their mind. It is important that at this level you remain positive and intend for the best results for all involved (win-win). This is very powerful, and anything less than the highest of motives will cause a tremendous karmic return to you. Hold this beam of light for a few moments. Visualize yourself and this person(s) in an ideal relationship in your opinion, one in which you both are able to express yourself clearly, and one of harmony and support for each other's positions and viewpoints. If you perform this exercise with someone with whom you have a conflict, take note that soon after this meditation you will nearly always see a dramatic change in the person's attitude toward you—for the better!

Keep in mind that the result of this meditation/ healing may not be an ideal relationship, but will nearly always result in immediate improvement, clearer communications, and instant reduction in conflict. If you anticipate a conflict or any type of impasse to occur in an upcoming meeting, perform the following exercise. This one brings all of those attending the meeting into the light.

Get yourself focused. See all of the members in the meeting coming to an agreeable solution to all of the problems and/or issues that need to be discussed. Visualize a sphere of pure light over the group. See a light field descend from this sphere and surround all of the members completely with this light. Know that this light will bring wisdom, clarity, and balance to any group.

Make it your intention that all in attendance will experience a win/win result. Accept the actual results as being of the highest good for all.

If you are ever in a meeting of any type and the energy gets wacky, scattered, or simply negative, immediately pull in this sphere of light over the center of the group. Ask that a resolution come, and that a win-win situation prevail. Sit back and watch the dynamics of the meeting change for the better.

Personal Relationships

As discussed above, personal relationships are the most power-ful for our emotions and the most common of all arenas of karma. If you can learn to heal one difficult relationship, then the others will be much easier. The meditation below will help greatly to that end. Sometimes the results are instant, other times the results take a little longer, depending on the nature of the karma, all those involved, and your capacity to work from the High Self and with real forgiveness and love. Remember that most individuals on the planet came into this life with the intention of balancing their personal karma. Consequently, this process represents the majority of the challenges we face and the work we must all complete.

Key to this meditative process is eliminating, as much as possible, your personal feelings of anger, hurt, resentment, emptiness, etc. Stay as nonjudgmental as possible—yes, it is possible. You will also need to stand back and look honestly and objectively at yourself. Take time to focus on all of the pos-itive qualities of yourself and the other person. Put energy into these positive areas and you will experience positive results. This can usually be done best through meditating and invok-ing your High Self, your spiritual guides, and asking Source to assist you in your relationship healing.

Personal Relationship Meditation

As in the previous meditation, ask to communicate with your friend's High Self from your High Self. See a beam of brilliant white light connecting your mind with theirs. Detach yourself as much as possible from your feelings, even if only for a few moments, and send them only positive thoughts. Feel free to pray to Source for help and support at this juncture.

Mentally tell this person that you forgive them completely for anything they may have done to intentionally harm you. Then say, "I forgive myself totally for feeling this way, and for doing anything intentionally to harm (your friend's name)." Then say, "I love and forgive you, I love and forgive myself."

See the two of you communicating clearly and openly without any negative or turbulent feelings. Visualize only a positive outcome. See the two of you sharing, laughing, and having fun together. Visualize your new relationship surrounded in an energy field of white light.

Keep in mind that this will help transmute the karma from this relationship, but this doesn't mean that the relationship will necessarily continue—continuing it may not be for the best interest, or highest good, of the two involved. There also may still need to be many elements that must be worked out in your everyday lives, such as a lengthy discussion at some time between the two of you (or away from each other), etc. As with every major issue in our life, patience and perseverance work the best in resolving personal relationship issues. Common sense cannot be overlooked as well. Many relationships are saved, or at least improved, through the process of professional counseling. Bringing a third party, an objective professional, to your situation may work the best in helping to heal your relationship. *To change any relationship you must first change your consciousness—your attitude. When you shift your attitude, you draw newer, more positive relationships to you. Again, the law of attraction is at work in all areas of your life.*

Remember that we tend to project our habits and faults onto others, especially those close to us. Before we criticize others, we need to reevaluate our own consciousness. Once we have done that, our personal relationships will improve dramatically. They will indeed become the greatest joys in our life!

Financial Healing

It is no secret that many suffer the stresses and strains of financial problems. Even though this isn't considered a disease or an illness, this struggle nevertheless gets reflected in our lives by symptoms such as: loss of energy, lack of motivation, depression, loss of confidence, lack of freedom, and all of the usual symptoms of stress. For complete health, *making one whole again,* balance is key—this includes financial balance. Financial abundance and the lack of financial stress in one's life must be part of the equation for this balance, real happiness, and the means to live a creative, fulfilling life. In this respect it may serve us well to address it in a similar manner as disease or affliction, especially when one considers the amount of time and energy most people spend achieving this financial balance.

For those who have spent much of their life, or at least a fair amount of time on their spiritual path, their focus has not been placed on making money. Again, *energy follows thought,* so venturing onto a serious spiritual quest diverts our energy, somewhat, away from a purely material existence. This is good in the sense that the material world, with all of its allure, is not an end unto itself. Often the result is that individuals find themselves growing and expanding dramatically within their own spiritual consciousness, but struggling to balance their checkbook. One cause of this lies in the focus of energy mentioned above. The second is that, in most cases, if one were to be infinitely abundant, they would tend to spend all of their time managing, spending, and protecting their money. Why would anyone in a position of financial wealth and success choose to go inward? Remember that we *chose* the families and the environment in which we wanted to be raised and learn our life's experience as a youth.

The outer distraction of financial wealth is a great temptation for nearly anyone. The sense of material fulfillment is too often complete and the outer life usually too preoccupied with materialism to consider a spiritual path. Recall in Chapter I the analogy of the diver, and the allure of the deep's treasures. If we are too attached to our possessions, many times life will take away our material belongings with the purpose of forcing us to look inward for our fulfillment and our happiness. Life has a mysterious way of showing us our lessons.

All of life here on Earth is an opportunity for growth. If we choose spiritual growth, our daily lives will provide us this opportunity. Sometimes this means a temporary loss or reduction of material possessions.

Sometimes our consciousness views the purchasing of anything as being wrong unless the Universe agrees. In other words, we often carry from our childhood a sense of always having to get approval or an okay from our parents that it's all right to purchase something. This need for approval many times gets transferred to the Universe or to a God who is watching over us. We have all the tools within us to manifest financial abundance in our lives—there is never a "God" or Spirit who is judging what we should or shouldn't have.

As a suggestion for self-healing your financial shortcomings or lack of material success, it may help to reevaluate just what you would like more of in your life in material terms. Look at the essence of what your object of desire will bring you. Energize the positive qualities you want to manifest in your life. Look at the quality of life you would like, not necessarily the quantity of things you would own.

The Universe supports our desire for a quality life. Quality should always be the desired outcome. Quantity may support our vision or manifestation of quality, but it does not necessarily equal quality.

A number of books and articles address finances and abundance, ranging from a purely material vantage point to a purely spiritual one. We won't expound any further in this text on the subject, but you will find throughout this text a variety of affirmations relating to healing. Use them also for your own financial abundance—substitute where you see fit terms such as "financial healing," "abundance," etc.

One final note on finances. There is no real reason why we should not experience financial abundance and freedom. For us to be happy and stress free, this critical area in our life must be resolved. One cannot achieve his or her purpose in life, nor be creative and productive, without basic financial security—it's part of our *pie graph of life!*

The Meditation Process

We've discussed a number of affirmations, visualization techniques, and meditations in the preceding pages. As with everything else, the only real way to be successful with these techniques is to begin to practice them. There are many applications of these tools, especially the art of meditation.

Generally, our Western culture perceives meditation as a type of passive, mystical, or even a strange, escape-oriented experience. This perspective is the result of a Westernized, and somewhat limited, intellectual mind. Some refer to this as our left-brain, or logical element, that is often so dominant in our modern society. Meditation can utilize all of the elements of the mind, and can assist us in transcending the limitations of our daily thought process. Many of those who scoff at others who do indeed have an interest in meditation, or in metaphysical thought, are simply in fear of their own nature. The inner process of continued meditation brings to the surface our inner self and the untapped potentials, which lie dormant within all of us. Our Western culture generally avoids this type of introspection. *We need balance in our inner and outer life, and meditation is a great facilitator to that end.*

While it's true that many people use meditation for peace, serenity, and relaxation, meditation can take many forms, reaping many rewards. It is simply a tool that can supplement almost any aspect of our life, from finding peace within and

> *Meditation is the primary tool for all self-healing techniques.*

understanding the deeper meaning of life, to manifesting a new place of residence or sleeping better. The image of an Indian guru sitting for hours in complete silence and complacency reflects only a small percentage of possible usage for this powerful process, not to mention the fact that, in our busy society, who has the time to spend hours each day in meditation?

There is much to be said, however, about the Eastern approach to meditation relevant to mind control. The Zen monks' practice of spending hours each day simply sitting and watching their breath represents a mental discipline we do not possess in our Western world. Discipline of the mind is difficult, yet extremely important—not only for all of the areas of healing and meditation, but for success in all areas of our lives.

Our minds tend to race out of control. We seek fulfillment in nearly every arena in life except for the quietude and bliss within our own being. More than ever before, the art of meditation could help us individually and collectively to calm our nerves, relax our minds, and tap into our Higher Self—our higher potentials. The meditation experience can also bring us into a dynamic balance within ourselves physically, emotionally, and mentally. With practice it can help us solve almost any problem or situation in our life.

For the sake of summarizing, let's capture all of the previous techniques of visualization and affirmation, and place them under the umbrella of meditation. Many would not categorize these processes this way, but it will help us make a convenient summary. From now on, when we mention meditation, we mean the general process of sitting or lying quietly and going within ourselves with a conscious, specific intent in mind. By the way, meditation has a primary difference from hypnotism: in meditation *the individual is completely under control at all times.* In hypnotism, one allows another to guide him or her into a state of unawareness, or into the subconscious. Hypnotism has its place, but we won't use it in this text on healing.

Continuing below and on the following pages is a brief summary of some of the general processes and uses of meditation, with the emphasis on the healing applications.

Concentration

Simple concentration is an active process in which one focuses the thoughts on a primary object. This object can be a picture in the mind's eye, following the rhythmic patterns of breathing, a simple thought of a previous experience, etc. When your mind is able to concentrate for a few minutes at a time without allowing intrusive thoughts to overshadow the concentration, then you are ready to move forward and experience the finer areas of meditation.

Concentration is critical for success in all areas of our lives. Professionals of all trades, engineers, scientists, athletes, etc., all know how to stay focused on their work.

One way to start learning to concentrate is to choose an object that you can easily visualize. Pick one about which you have little or no feelings—say a fruit, or a tree, or a picture—so that your emotions do not enter into the process. Simply get comfortable, close your eyes, and bring that image into your mind's eye. As thoughts enter, calmly bring your focus back to the image you have chosen. If you feel that the thought needs some attention, simply tell yourself that you will give it attention later, but not now. Sometimes it's helpful to have a writing pad next to you so you can jot down any unusual thoughts or experiences. *All thoughts are valid!* Never judge yourself for a negative thought! In reality, there are no negative or positive thoughts. Start to become the detached observer to your thoughts. When you can do this, you have reached a new plateau in your consciousness. Concentration will start as an active process, but eventually it becomes more *passive*. The activities of the mind soon become still and the process becomes effortless.

Sometimes lighting a candle and visualizing the candle flame is also an easy way to start to focus internally. Meditating in nature is a great place to start because of the natural sounds. Also by simply sitting with eyes closed and following your breath, you can calm your thought process and begin to relax your mind, body, and emotions. Our thoughts and our breathing process are intimately connected—balancing one nearly always balances the other.

Meditation groups are a good way to help you get started. They provide positive, focused energy, which is necessary for the beginner. Also, I highly recommended that you experience a variety of forms and techniques of meditation before you settle into just one. Remember that in the end, you are your own teacher—no one can give you concentration, meditation, or enlightenment! It is up to you to develop it!

Affirmation

Affirmation is an active process, which energizes a specific, positive outcome by repeating a phrase many times. Repeating mentally, for example, *"I am healed,"* sets up that thought and feeling that reverberates through our conscious mind, our subconscious mind, our emotional body, and eventually our physical body. Utilizing strong, positive affirmations, one can choose any area of their life to heal: mental, physical, emotional, financial, relationships, etc. The process can be done verbally or mentally.

There are numerous affirmations throughout this text to draw on as examples. Remember to never limit yourself in terms of what you can manifest in your life through affirmation, especially in the arena of healing. And remember the three key elements in healihng: faith, intention, and the belief in a greater Power.

Your affirmation may be general or specific. A specific example is: *"I am manifesting a perfect spinal column."* We have already discussed affirmation and visualization in much depth previously, so we're just summarizing somewhat at this point.

Visualization

Visualization is another active process in which the mind forms a specific thought for a specific outcome. In this form of meditation, one gets quiet and begins forming a picture in his or her mind of the desired outcome—for example, a perfect body part. The thought is empowered when coupled with positive, dynamic emotions. Thoughts of this nature must be of the highest intent, and must be as specific and clear as possible. Remember, energy follows thought. Whatever you focus upon will surely manifest. The visualization process is the most direct proof of this law.

Affirmation combined with visualization is much more powerful than either one individually. When one holds a thought (visualize) of a healed or perfect area of their life, and combines that with an accompanying affirmation, the results are much faster. For example, in the previous affirmation, *"I am manifesting a perfect spinal column,"* holding the mental picture of a perfect spinal column filled with radiant white light will attract amazing healing energy to you. This is much more challenging, but much more effective. Always invoke your High Self, or Soul, to support you in your healing efforts.

It's somewhat of a cliché, but true, that the ultimate experience in visualization is to become one with the thought.

Contemplation

Contemplation is a more passive process than those above. This form of meditation has been used for thousands of years in the Eastern cultures for understanding the deeper wisdom and knowledge of life. In this process one must quiet the mind and become receptive to the inner, deeper levels within. If you want a specific answer on most any subject, or an insight into a situation in your life, you can use contemplation for this understanding. In reality, it is true that the answer always lies within, but the mind must be calmed to discover this knowledge. Answers of this type do not come from the logically-oriented, busy mind. They come from the more subtle level, the intuitive mind.

It is all right to get advice, counseling, and guidance from others, but one must always use their own intuition and best judgment when making decisions, or even when forming a sense of what truth is. The process of discerning the truth has never been more critical than in our current period of time. With so much written material on the market; i.e., predictions of all types, channeling, new health modalities, etc., pulling out the truth of a teaching is no longer a simple task. Contemplation, the art of going within and becoming very still, can help tremendously to get at the truth of a teaching, and guide one to the real inner wisdom and understanding.

Over the past twenty years or so, the process of spiritual channeling and psychic counseling has become quite popular, and even fashionable in some circles. This is all well and good for some, since it can often provide a perspective on one's life that is objective and from a much broader viewpoint. However one must always be cautious in this highly diversified and somewhat undeveloped field. Many individuals claiming to be channels of higher beings and *Masters*, are bringing in information that is sometimes mundane, incorrect, and merely reflects aspects from within their own being. Even the best-intentioned people can unknowingly misguide you. Again, use your intuition and common sense. *Remember, the answer lies within!*

One way to begin the process of contemplation is to take a beautiful flower, such as a rose, and hold it in front of you. Think of all the aspects that this rose represents to you: the scent, the color, the overall beauty. Taking this technique further, contemplate the underlying essence this flower provides you. What does this rose bring to you? Are there qualities in this flower that you adore? What is your experience? How do you *feel* about this flower? Do you experience a oneness with this rose?

In a similar manner, you can take a concept or question and focus internally on it, discovering many things about it that you never thought of previously. The key is being able to find a quiet time and place to do this, and being able to stay focused on the subject for a period of time. Inner contemplation of this type is truly rare among individuals in our busy world, yet so drastically needed. This is the most challenging form of mediation, yet the most rewarding. Many people are unknowingly seeking and thirsting for this experience.

An interesting byproduct of the process of contemplation is receiving insight at a later time. You may think, ponder, or contemplate on a subject for a long time, yet receive no direct insight. Later, perhaps driving down the freeway, or sitting in the movie theater, you may have a flash of insight into your thought. The mind is always at work, especially the subconscious and superconscious. The answer you're looking for is always there; it just needs to filter to your conscious mind.

One way to begin the inner process of contemplation is to start the concentration exercise and expand upon it. After your thoughts are quieted, start with the object, but explore it totally, asking questions as in the example of the rose. Ask your High Self to provide you the answers you are looking for—be patient and they will come.

Sending Healing to Others

This is another active process in which we bring in, using visualization, an individual at a distance who needs healing. We simply ask the Higher Power to allow us to be channels for healing and then call this person's name. It helps if we visualize the person and surround them in a beautiful white light field. Intention is the key. If we have developed our ability to concentrate and visualize, our healing at a distance is empowered greatly. Once you have worked a little with the techniques in this text, you can draw to you those who are at a distance and perform the same type of healing as if they were standing in front of you.

Simply getting quiet and saying a prayer for the individual sends a powerful healing energy to them. *Absent healing,* or *healing at a distance* is a process that incorporates the same principles as healing others and ourselves who are present. The only difference is that their physical body is not present. Through our intention, concentration, and will, we eliminate the distance, and healing can occur.

To start this process, simply ask to be a healing channel for a specific person. Mentally bring this person to you and surround them in pure light, then begin to mentally send healing energy to them. If there were something specific you would do if they were present, go ahead and do it. The only difference is that you are working in other dimensions than the physical. It greatly helps to count to ten as you bring the person to you, then count backward, ten to one, when you are finished. This sends the healing energy back and helps reestablish their perfect pattern. This form of healing transcends time and space. It is proof that we have an existence that is not bound by the three-dimensional, material world of time/space. (See Chapter II for an in-depth meditation on absent healing.)

Manifestation

The active process of manifestation is simply a broader, more expansive visualization. In the context of this book, we have been emphasizing healing energies and how to use them. Once we have learned the tools of visualization and affirmation, we can incorporate them in all areas of our life. In self-healing, our visualization is focused inwardly toward ourselves, and sometimes outwardly to others. In manifesting other needs in our life, such as a new residence, or a more dependable car, our visualization is energized and sent outward to the world as a specific thought form, which satisfies a need in our life.

Section
39

Section
38

EXTREMITIES
GOVERNING
LEFT

23

EXTREMITIES
GOVERNING
RIGHT

22

THE
ETHERIC
DIAMOND

For example, if you need a new vehicle to get you around, you can go into a relaxed meditation and focus on your need. Ponder the positive outcome of a new vehicle—what would it add to your life? How would your life be enriched by it? How would it boost your self-esteem if you owned this car?

After you have done this, and you're convinced that you need this vehicle *and that you deserve it,* you're ready to put the thought out there. One way to do this is to see yourself sitting and driving in a new vehicle that serves all of your needs. You can envision a specific car or truck, or simply feel yourself in one that serves your needs. Feel good about this! Know that you deserve this!

In your mind's eye, surround your thought in radiant light energy. Gently, but firmly, send that thought out to the universe for manifestation.

Remember—energy follows thought, and *focused thought* of good intention, along with *positive emotion,* is the most powerful tool we have. If your desired outcome changes, simply change your thought, and resend it. It's like an architect who revises and fine-tunes his design. *You are the architect of your life.* Your present thoughts are creating the reality for your future.

To complete your manifestation, simply start looking around on the physical plane for your desire. You will be amazed how easy it is now that you have sent out the energized thought. Don't forget we are living in a material world. In our environment, we always need to take some action at the physical level, regardless of the size or type of our manifestation. With some practice, the action required at the physical level, such as checking out a newspaper ad, becomes minimal. If you perform this technique and are still unsuccessful, rest assured that it is not quite time for your desired manifestation.

torso, and eventually out the bottoms of your feet. See yourself as a conduit, or pipe, for this uplifting, vibrant energy to flow through. See yourself sitting in an invisible cylinder and allow this colorful energy to fill up this cylinder, which extends two to three feet around you in all directions. As you relax into the feeling and experience of the color with which you are working, the process becomes passive.

The effects of using this type of color meditation are enhanced greatly if you understand the general quality of the color *essence*, if you can hold a general thought of the color, and, more importantly, if you can feel the color, the energy, as it comes into your body. Below is a very general and brief description of some of the basic colors and the qualities they can bring into your life, especially when used in a meditation/visualization. These basic qualities can also be brought into your energy field through the clothes that you wear and the colors with which you surround yourself in your homes and work areas.

Red: Red represents the basic life force. It is grounding and helps the individual connect to the physical plane. Red is a great energy to bring in for periods of lack of motivation, for inspiration, and for physical energy. It helps greatly also for enhancing our will power and determination. It brings warmth to the body.

Orange: Orange represents vitality and cheerfulness. Anyone with a majority of orange in their energy field will be very alive, with lots of energy. Orange helps with depression and assists us in energizing our thoughts as well as our bodies. Bring orange into internal organs that need healing and energizing. Orange is excellent for uplifting us emotionally, and it enhances our natural immune system.

Yellow: Yellow is another color of vitality, but of a more subtle nature, bringing vibrant energy to the emotions and mental activity. Professionals and mentalists who engage their minds a majority of the time have much yellow around them. Yellow is good for clarity of all types—physical, emotional, and mental. To overcome sluggish thought processes, bring in yellow, flooding the mental body.

Green: Green is the great healer and balancer. Nature exudes the color, vibrancy, and energy of green. For any illness or imbalance, bring a brilliant shade of Kelly green into your entire energy field. Feel it heal your body, and balance all the other levels. Whenever possible, go to the woods and allow those physical shades and tones of green to seep into your energy field and heal and balance all of the subtle areas of your body, mind, and emotions.

Blue: Blue is a great color for spirituality. It can also bring into your energy field a creative, expressive quality. Use blue when you want to expand your consciousness, express yourself better, and uplift your vibrations. Blue can assist your willpower and help you in understanding your greater purpose in life. Blue has a general calming effect on the energy field.

Light Blue: Use light blue when you are mentally or emotionally very scattered and need to get focused. This calms down and integrates various levels of the energy field. This is a very soothing energy, and can help you fall asleep at night. Sky blue is also a great healer for the nervous system.

Indigo: This color is used to assist those upon the spiritual path to awaken to the spiritual mind in the forehead area, or *third eye*. Indigo can integrate your energy on the mental levels and bring deep understanding and knowledge with it.

Violet: Violet is also associated many times with spiritual awakening. This is the highest vibration of the blue spectrum and can help open one of the many spiritual abilities—clairvoyance, intuition, etc. Violet has a very transmutative quality. When used for this purpose, it can actually help to transmute, transform, and burn away negative karma and any blockage that may prevent the individual from expanding and moving forward with his or her life.

Purple: Purple is another spiritual color. It is extremely useful when focused on the emotional body. In this application it helps to calm and integrate scattered emotions. Our emotions are a tool that triggers our mind to understand and process our life's lessons. Purple helps bring this understanding and integration to our mind and our emotions. Purple brings a deep reverence for God with it. Many pictures and paintings of Christ show him wearing purple.

Silver: Silver is associated with communication, clarity, and multidimensionality. Silver can be used mentally as a silver bubble around our energy field to protect against negative influences. It acts as a filter, and not as a shield. Silver can also be brought into the aura by a healer to help dissolve tumors or any unwanted growth. It can purge the entire energy field, releasing all undesired elements in the body.

Gold: Gold typically represents wisdom and enlightenment. When used in healing it can help in many ways. In self-healing and meditation, gold quickens the spiritual mind and the Christ within. When brought into the physical body it can bring great healing to the cellular level and even bring regeneration and complete recovery to the body, to a system, to an organ, etc. Gold is uplifting and facilitates the merging of our personality with our spiritual, or High Self. Gold brings with it the feelings of love, wisdom, and enlightenment.

Reddish-Brown: Browns and grays should generally be avoided in healing. They typically represent energy that is a muddied -up version of the purer colors—sometimes resentment, sometimes hatred, etc. However to assist you in getting grounded to Earth, bright and clear Earth browns can help. Be certain when you bring in brown that it is a more reddish hue than a dark hue, and feel it to be very vibrant and radiant. Feel it connecting you to the Earth and grounding your energies, especially through your feet.

White: All color comes from the one white light. We can always bring in the white light for upliftment, protection, and healing. Feel the light as it enters your aura and uplifts and charges each and every cell in your body. When working with another, use the white light for protection and healing. If in doubt as to which color to use either for yourself or for another, the white light can always be used. Use it to heal, clear areas, and bring *light* and clarity to a situation. The spiritual beings working with you (and we all have them) can assist you much easier when you have invoked the white Light of Protection and you work with the light consciously. Invoking the white light must be a prerequisite to any type of healing work.

Healing a Situation

Within certain minor limitations we have the ability to correct, change, or transmute each and every event in our life—past, present, or future. Healing is not limited to only a present situation or an imperfection in our physical body.

As we have already discovered, relationships, whether personal or professional, can be healed. Situations such as past decisions or past actions can also be corrected or healed, thereby changing and healing the present. This is because when we work with this type of energy, we project ourselves beyond time in the present, linear sense.

Each and every aspect of our life has the potential for perfection.

To bring about a positive event in the future, simply bring into focus a current situation you would like to see result in a positive, *win-win* outcome. This can be a relationship, a business agreement, etc. It's important when *seeing* your positive outcome that you do not infringe, or disrupt, someone else's path or life in any way. A win-win means all parties receive a benefit and are happy with the outcome, and you are not imposing your personal will upon another. When you are certain that you are not negatively interfering with another, then visualize the perfect outcome you desire and surround it in light. It's really that simple! As with all other processes, it will take a little practice to perfect. Use any or all of the previously described techniques for your visualization. However, you will find that success is inevitable, even with your first attempts. It would be very helpful to go over the previous section on concentration and visualization.

If you have made a past decision that affects you today in a negative or limiting way, and you wish you had not made that decision, it can be changed also, but extreme care must be taken! If you go back in time, and change a decision, the ramifications may be drastic! Before you attempt this technique, go through all the possible implications and possibilities of your new decision. Ask Source for guidance and for the outcome to be for your highest good. This is one area of visualization that requires extreme caution.

In the realities that we are discussing, linear time, as we use it in our daily lives, is nonexistent. Therefore, when we change a *past* decision, we are simply changing our mind, so to speak. There may be events that result from changing the mind, but those events will in turn manifest in the present. In essence, the past and the present merge into the *now* experience. The past could mean a decision that I made this morning as I made my coffee and chose to use some milk that turned out to be soured. Or, it could represent a lifetime in A.D. 727 when I chose not to marry my lover of many years and ended up getting killed, leaving the relationship unresolved, and my lover distraught, empty, and angry. Both are equally accessible by my consciousness. Both can be changed to a great degree.

The past is a pocket of experience in our minds, our emotions, our energy field—in our consciousness. We have the ability to go into this pocket and change it. For example, if I was in the checkout line at the grocery store, and I decided not to purchase a certain brand of coffee, I could leave the line and go exchange it for the brand I desired. As I returned to the checkout line, the dynamics there may be the same, or they may be quite different. The line may be gone, or it may be longer. The dynamics of the checkout line represents the present again, but the real issue is that I am feeling better and more fulfilled because I have corrected my decision. I now have the coffee I want, and I will leave the store happier. No doubt that linear time (time on my watch) has passed, but now my present time feels better because I went back and corrected a decision.

This is a crude but useful example. My trip to exchange the coffee represents my reaching back in the pocket of my consciousness. In our consciousness, it wouldn't matter if this trip were to take us back five minutes or five centuries. Each of these pockets of the past is equally accessible by our Higher Self.

The primary effect of changing the past is upon your own emotional body. Events and other individuals may be affected somewhat, although not always, but since you are the one making the change—seeing it, feeling it—you are the one who will experience the most results. A byproduct of making a change in a past action or decision is the release or balance of karma with others, because nearly all of our karma (cause-and-effect energy) is with other people. By making a change for the better in a past situation, you have released not only some of your own karmic burden, but also some karma for all of those involved.

Here's one example of changing and transmuting a relationship. Say you are very good friends with someone of the opposite sex, and you have also been physically attracted to that person. Over time, you get to know the person very well, and both of you sense that a personal relationship would probably never work in the long run. You think it over. You decide to get involved anyway romantically, knowing the probably outcome.

After a short time, the inevitable happens—you are very compatible physically, but mentally and emotionally, it is not a good match. Feelings are hurt. The friendship is severely damaged. You know it will never be the same.

To soften this shock and to heal the friendship, changing your past decision will certainly help. Take some time alone and go back to the moment you made the decision to go ahead and become involved. See yourself making that decision. Now go back in time a few moments prior to that—back to the time you were processing the possibilities. This time, decide not to become involved in any way except as a friend. *See yourself telling your friend of this decision, and feel it. Surround this vision in light, and release it to the Universe.* Ask that this decision not harm anyone else. You will be surprised at the emotional healing that will follow. Your friendship may never be quite the same, but there will always be a great improvement.

Keep in mind that not all decisions that we may think were wrong ones were actually wrong. Many times we think a decision is wrong because we are not seeing it from the big picture.

If there is such a thing as a mistake, it is to keep making decisions that are not for our highest good, or deciding to repeat the same old experiences, which we don't like and which limit us. These types of decisions do limit our experience and our spiritual growth is thwarted.

From the greater perspective of our soul progression, there are no mistakes!

Most of these latter types of patterns do not require a meditation in changing the past, but simply exercising common sense in the pattern of our daily life. It's important also not to waste unnecessary time going over the past. Simply look at these issues objectively and know that all can be changed. Most aspects of our lives can be changed simply by changing our thought patterns and actions in the present, and not by consciously changing anything in our past. Common sense and practicality always have their place.

Sending Light Through Time

We have discussed healing a situation and a relationship. There are healing processes that involve specific situations in specific time slots. In a similar manner, we can choose to send light to a general *time slot*. This gives us a time period, say a day, for example, in which we focus our light with positive thoughts, intentions, and outcomes. I have personally found this to be an extremely helpful process, especially if I know I'm facing an extremely difficult day.

For example, in my morning meditation (or even during my morning shower) I will choose to send a brilliant white light through the entire day ahead of me. I envision all of the major events of which I am aware being surrounded in this light, with great results coming to them all. I ask that this light uplift me, provide me energy for the day, and give me guidance for all the situations that may arise unexpectedly. I also ask that all those with whom I come into contact be uplifted by this light. I send this light through the entire day ahead of me.

This process really works. It provides us a focus for a day, a week, or even just a few minutes or hours. The shorter the time span, the more focused our light can be. As a start, I would suggest using a period of no more than one day at a time. You will see great results with this process, especially for those of you who have a busy schedule, with many unscheduled and unforeseen events appearing in your daily life. Other applications could be vacations, business trips, or family gatherings.

Light of Protection

There appears to be a certain magical process that occurs when one calls forth the Light of Protection. This phrase invokes the spiritual energies, which have supported and protected millions of souls over great expanses of Earth time. It has the power not only to protect, but also to uplift the vibrations of anyone. Called forth, it can be sustained for quite a length of time. It is suggested that one invoke it at least once each day, especially in the morning, prior to going out to greet the world.

While in meditation, simply say mentally, "I call forth the light of protection to protect me now and forevermore from all elements not for my highest good." It helps if you visualize a cylinder of white light descending from overhead and filling up your entire energy field. This would extend for a few feet in all directions.

It is important to use this same invocation prior to any type of individual group work involving meditation and healing energy. It is literally a requirement for the safe transference of healing energy in a one-on-one situation.

Silver Bubble

Dr. Trevor Creed from Australia first introduced the *silver bubble* to me. He uses it in his healing work to protect himself as well as his client, and also to help seal the client's energy field so that energy does not *leak* out. The silver bubble is not a totally insulated shield, but rather a fine-mesh filter that allows our energy field to breathe, while filtering out negative energies.

Simply call forth to your High Self to surround yourself in the silver bubble. It helps greatly if you can visualize yourself surrounded in this bubble of silver, extending outside your body by a few feet in all directions. Using the silver bubble each morning is recommended, along with the Light of Protection. In Chapter V, we'll look more closely at the silver bubble, as well as other specific techniques of this powerful tool of Chironic Healing.

Violet Flame Meditation

I personally have used the *Violet Flame Meditation* for over twenty years and have found it to be extremely effective for uplifting my energy, accelerating my growth, and releasing old patterns that no longer serve me on my path.

In metaphysical terminology, the violet flame is an action from a certain spiritual energy (Seventh Ray) and embraces the process of total transmutation. In simpler terms, this is a manifestation of the *Law of Forgiveness*, which in turn is based on the *Law of Love*. When we begin to experience Universal love, we experience transformation of our personality and all aspects of our life. In this process of growth, spiritual laws, such as the manifestation of the violet flame, can help tremendously in our transformation process and the acceleration of our growth. In theory, the violet flame *transmutes* all the elements in our energy field, whether they are physical, emotional, or mental. Transmutation is a process that clears or burns out the old, leaving only the new, purer, and fresher elements behind.

The ancient alchemists, so history records, had the ability to change base metals into gold. This was a type of chemical transmutation, but the real transmutation is the evaporation of our baser human traits, leaving behind only the shining, clear essence of our Soul, or our *golden self.* Setting up this violet energy in your energy field not only begins this transmutative process, but also brings with it the higher frequencies of Spirit, augmenting your every step along the path of life.

Meditation

Get yourself grounded as in the previous meditations.
Call forth the action of the seventh ray, or simply say,
"I call forth the Violet Flame." Visualize your entire

energy field, three to four feet in all directions, being consumed by this beautiful flame of violet energy.

Hold this flame in your energy field. If you like, call to the Master St. Germain to assist you in this effort. He is the "keeper" of this flame. Feel this energy. It should feel cool and calming. Know that it is working at deep levels to heal, transform, and transmute your life for your higher good.

This brief affirmation can assist you also:

I am a being of the violet fire, I am the purity of God's desire.

Repeat this affirmation several times, feeling the rhythm each time, while mentally holding the flame in your mind's eye. When you begin to feel the flame and the color engulf you, know that transformation and healing is taking place. The violet flame is a great tool for releasing karma. The effects of even just one in-depth meditation on the violet flame can last for months and even years.

Limitations

We've covered many methods and perspectives on self-healing in this chapter. Indeed much more can be done with nearly everyone in terms of self-improvement and self-healing. The mind is an amazing vehicle, and in our current phase of evolution, it is vastly misunderstood and untapped. It can set into motion great events, total health, happiness, and success in our lives, or it can guide us nowhere, except into ignorance, disease, and deceit. It is the director of our consciousness—how we use it is up to us.

Yet there are times when we all need outside facilitators—those who can move our energy and help us heal ourselves. A rough analogy is a cup of coffee with cream and sugar—it needs to be stirred—it cannot stir itself. By stirring it we have not changed its fundamental composition. We have simply mixed and blended the separate ingredients into one solution.

We are similar to that cup of coffee. We often cannot stir ourselves. We sometimes need that outside force to blend and align our separated and fragmented energy field(s). Let's now look at some of the fundamentals of healing others.

I am a balanced instrument of my Soul,
I am integrated within my physical, mental,
and emotional expressions.
I am clear to be what I am. I am Light.

IV

Principles in Healing Others

There are few joys in life greater than the joy of healing another human being. It really doesn't matter whether you are providing them emotional support during a crisis, listening intimately to their immediate issue, assisting them with a laying on of hands session, or channeling healing energy for a physical ailment. The feeling of love and the fulfilling sensation of service when we heal another are unsurpassed by most experiences in our lives.

When we heal with our heart, we are in complete alignment with this principle. The process of healing another individual is uplifting beyond comparison, attracting energy, love, and light to the healer as well as the one being healed. Often, while healing someone, I personally experience a blissful energy, unlike anything else. The only experience that I personally could compare this with would be witnessing the births of my three children.

There is indeed a magical chemistry of energetic exchange that takes place during the healing process. It exudes a spiritual quality and a merging of essences unlike any other experience in our world. Both the healer and the one being healed share this great energy exchange.

> *It is the nature of the Soul to serve others. When you are serving, your energy, wisdom, and sense of purpose are all enhanced greatly with Universal Energy.*
>
> ◆
>
> *As healers, we are facilitators for another's self-healing process—we are helping others help themselves.*

Learning and understanding how to heal yourself is the greatest possible teacher in learning to heal others. The obvious difference is that we are directing our healing energy outside ourselves, and the dynamics change dramatically because we now have two energy fields interrelating rather than one by itself.

Tremendous results are available through self-healing, and it is also a fact that many times a second facilitator is required to assist in the healing process, moving and realigning the patient's energy pattern.

When we heal others, we are acting as agents for healing, or *conduits for energy*. Sometimes this role becomes that of a catalyst, sometimes as a balancer, or sometimes we heal simply by listening and being available for the *inner workers* and the subtle energies to do their work.

Healing can take place in an infinite variety of ways and does not necessarily require the process of placing your hands on or near someone who has a physical problem. However, the use of the hands and mind to direct energy to another will be the primary focus in this chapter and the next.

The Soul Is the Healer

If you accept the basic identity structure mentioned in Chapter II, then you know that we have a Higher or Greater Self (Soul) that generally exists just beyond our normal, waking consciousness—at a somewhat higher vibration, if you will. This aspect of ourselves is the element that determines when our lessons are learned and plots our general plan in life, while at the same time providing the environment for these lessons and, in general, for our life experiences. Always keep in mind that this same paradigm is true for your client as well. *His or her health and general well-being are a reflection of their total life path and how he or she has been able to adapt to life's challenges.* For example, it should be obvious that a very stressed-out person is not handling life very well. They are not working in harmony with their Soul urges. The result is usually poor health and low vitality.

As healers, we are being asked to assist this Soul in recovering their energy, getting focused, and becoming whole again. They have chosen their lifestyle and their lessons in life. We cannot judge this or change it—we are simply helping them meet their challenges with balance, and, as much as possible, freeing them from pain.

There is usually a very specific reason why a certain person was guided to you for healing. Your modality, personality, spiritual evolvement, or simply your energy is what your client needs. *There are no mistakes in this process.* People are naturally drawn specifically to you for a reason, especially if you work in the health field. It is the law of attraction at work again. As we mentioned earlier, *each and every occasion that you facilitate healing for yourself or another, you also open the doors of opportunity for growth and expansion—both for*

you and your client. Love must be the basis for all of your heal-
ing work.

You must keep the concept of the soul and of its lessons in mind during your work, especially when working with those who have serious, chronic afflictions. Not only are there major lessons to learn, but long-term problems take years to mani-fest, and usually have many layers of emotional patterns built upon them as well. Consequently, it will usually take some time to undo or heal the condition. We build our layers of blockages over time, like adding the skins of an onion over its core, and these layers typically do not all come off at once. The more *open* your client is to you and your modality, the more *effective* is the healing process you provide.

Each of us is totally unique, our paths are unique, and our challenges and imperfections are unique. We obviously need to address each of our clients in this manner without assum-ing anything. When we look at a symptom we should never generalize or assume the underlying cause.

In chronic conditions, it is best to approach the problem or imperfection from as many holistic perspectives as possible.

We must also always be open to all possible methodologies and/or modalities that can help another soliciting our assistance. I personal-ly have referred clients to an acu-puncturist, a massage therapist, and a naturopath, among others, to work in conjunction with my form of treatments. These combinations are only a few examples of many that work very well.

Taking this further, a variety of possible treatments can be applied in parallel to a lower back problem. To resolve the imperfection, we should ask how it got there. We may want to seek out a massage therapist, possibly try acupuncture, physical therapy, natural herbal relaxants, and seek chiropractic treatment. We may also use ice or a hot tub.

In addition, we could advise a client to visualize a perfect lower back, extremely mobile and flexible, as well as free from all pain (see the previous chapter). Many times the cause is stressful emotions, built up over time, and the resolution of this cause will ensure permanent treatment. Lower back pain at the mental/emotional level is often the result of financial stress. The point here is to consider a physical, emotional, and mental cure or treatment all in parallel with each other. In severe and/or chronic conditions, suggest a checkup from a qualified physician—never overlook the value of common sense.

When you are working on a subject, it is always best to discuss their situation thoroughly. From even a short chat you can gather volumes of information and insight into the cause of the affliction, while at the same time building a good confidence level with your client. Don't forget the basics from the previous chapter—balance of body, mind, and emotions. Activity, rest, and recreation are required, along with a balance of male/ female, active/passive energies.

It is also important to remember that most people respond better to some healing modalities than to others. For example, I personally respond very well to the methods of acupuncture and oriental medicine. I do not do well with antibiotics, or with traditional chiropractic adjustments. It's simply a matter of our body type (energy field), our attitude, and our overall disposition at the time of the treatment. A major factor in all modalities is the disposition, or "expectation," of the patient.

What worked for an individual in the past may no longer be a valuable technique, and what was out of the question twenty years ago as a treatment may now be the best treatment for the

We are energy. If your energy field shifts due to growth and change, the treatment or modality for healing will usually shift as well.

affliction. Never limit yourself or the one to be healed in terms of which modality or technique to incorporate. As we grow and change, methods affect us differently—some work better, while others may tend to have little or no effect on us. What was once a viable technique may no longer work at all, simply because the individual's energy has changed or shifted dramatically. Remember our opening comments. *We are energy*, and *as energy* we are changing, growing, and evolving, moment by moment.

Healing with Your Hands

There are many successful ways to heal another with the hands. One such modality, Chironic Healing, will be discussed in some detail in the next chapter, but there are some general concepts that will help anyone be able to facilitate healing in another, no matter what their background, training, or belief system may be. Here are some important points to remember:

◆ *Love* must be the basis in all forms of healing—it is the real key to success and the doorway to infinite energy.

◆ Always *clear* and *protect* the area where you are working.

◆ Always *be as clear and balanced as possible yourself* before you attempt to work on another. Never work when you are overstressed, depressed, or tired.

◆ Remember the three guidelines to successful healing: *faith, intention, and belief in a Higher Power.*

♦ *Source will direct energy and healing to those areas which require healing,* even if you are not aware of them—and in ways which you may not consciously understand. When you trust in the process, your healing will be multidimensional, regardless of your own experience or knowledge.

Not only must you always protect the space in which you are doing your work, but you must always protect yourself. The best way to do this is to call forth the Light of Protection before each session, as well as to surround yourself and your client in the silver bubble of energy. This silver will filter out all of the unwanted or negative energy that approaches your field, allowing only positive, uplifting vibrations to enter each other's fields.

Many empathetic individuals who are involved in the field of healing actually take on the distorted energy of their clients. This is very common, but also very dangerous. It is really not the healer's responsibility to do this.

> *Always ask Source that you be a channel for healing. This assures your alignment with the patient's Soul and sets up the proper focus and intention.*
>
> ♦
>
> *It is not the healer's responsibility to experience or receive another's energy.*

If you do not detach yourself emotionally from your client, you will not only succumb to their energy, you will be of much less service to them. *There is a big difference between emotion and compassion.* One can have total compassion for another, yet not feel the emotions that the other is experiencing. This is a fine line to walk—not only in the healing field, but in life itself. It is perhaps one of our greatest challenges, both as healers and as human beings. *We must always be sensitive and compassionate to others, but we are not required to experience their experience.*

After you have performed your protection ceremony, ask that you not be allowed to take on another's energy. *It is that simple. Your intention and the Light of Protection will keep you from harm.* Your heart center must be open to facilitate healing, but your focus must remain in the forehead—this will keep you out of your solar plexus focus (the feeling center just above the navel), and out of trouble! This is also the reason you must always be balanced and clear before you start your work. The more out of balance you are, the more susceptible you become to another's energy.

Remember that if your energy is flowing in an outward fashion from your energy field to another, it is nearly impossible for another's energy to get into your field. It would be like trying to push water up a waterfall. The process of protection cannot be overemphasized, especially for those who are new to this field and those who are very sensitive to energy.

Seers and Feelers of Energy

There are generally two types of healers: *seers* and *feelers*. Most can do some of both. *Feeling-type* healers send much of their healing energy through their solar plexus area, as just mentioned, and through their heart center. The solar plexus is the area in which our emotions are processed and experienced, and greatly affects all of our abdominal organs, especially the digestive tract, spleen, pancreas, gall bladder, and liver.

We all know the feeling of being knotted up inside, or the hurt we feel when we've lost a loved one. That is energy in the solar plexus that is blocked and/or distorted. It is no longer flowing out, nor in balance. The solar plexus area is extremely sensitive, especially to spiritually evolved souls, and can become damaged quite easily if not properly protected. Again, always use the Light of Protection prior to working with another. Great healing can occur through this region, but great distress can be the result, as well, if one is not cautious.

As healers, it is especially important that we keep our emotional center clear. As channels we filter through our field to our client the healing energy which Source is providing. If we are distorted, we may distort that energy to our client in such a way as to not provide any healing energy at all. Only in rare cases can we actually harm another, because of our intention and the protective field of light we have set in place. It is possible, however, to harm ourselves if we are not properly protected, or if we are extremely tired.

When you have protected the area and the client, and after you have asked to be a channel for healing from Source, you have essentially protected the client from your energy. However, if you are not clear, or you are in an emotional state of turmoil, the client will not receive the healing properly. The

If you don't feel clear and balanced, don't allow yourself to enter another's energy field as a healing agent—it's that simple.

scattered energy will usually not directly affect him or her, but what often happens is the client will feel your *unbalanced* energy, or your uneasiness, and unconsciously or consciously shut down. When this happens, healing energy cannot flow. There are some situations in which a client can actually feel or pick up on your distorted energy field. Most of the time, they will not be a return client of yours!

When one is healing another, there is a synchronicity, an intimate interplay, that takes place at the energetic levels. It is important that the client feel totally comfortable and receptive to you; otherwise a complete dynamic interchange will not take place. In reality, the healing process starts as your soul merges with that of your client. During this subtle process you are providing healing energy multidimensionally, in ways and areas you may never consciously understand or even be aware of. These subtle energies, and the proper merging of fields, cannot take place if you are not clear and balanced.

Feeler-type healers use their feeling nature to sense not only the location of the problem areas, but to actually send healing energy. The detection or feeling sensation can be as basic as feeling hot or cold, sensing much energy or lack of energy, respectively, or it can be simply intuitive, such as feeling a need to send a specific color to a specific area.

You can practice this feeling sensation by having a friend sit in a side chair with their back to the side. Hold your hand just a few inches away from their body, palm toward them, and slowly move your hand along their spine. Close your eyes, and, moving your hand slowly, take note of what you feel. Be open to anything that you sense; you may be surprised at how sensitive you really are. Start first by feeling the energy with your hands. Then close your eyes, and feel what your intuition and feeling centers are telling you. Without judgment, simply watch and experience. As in all processes, this sensitivity will grow with practice.

Seer-type healers tend to be very visual and can see images of the energy patterns of the client. They can sometimes actually project themselves into an area of the client's body and *see* the problem, or the extent of a problem/blockage. They also have a great ability to project clear, positive thought forms to the client. This often happens at very subtle levels, but remember that subtle energy is the most powerful over time. Individuals who can visualize easily are also usually very good at self-healing.

Seer-type healers work primarily through the mind center, or the third-eye center, which lies in the center of the forehead. Many times when *looking* with your third eye into another's field, you may see things and patterns that are unworldly and quite odd. Don't be alarmed; the shapes, colors, and forms of energy patterns are infinite. You are not imagining things—you are seeing energy. Often Source will give you a certain shape or image to catch your attention. You should follow it with a healing technique appropriate for the problem.

In the practical sense, most healers incorporate both the tools of seeing and feeling the energy pattern. I personally tend to be intuitive and sometimes see energy patterns, while at other times I feel them as well. More often than not, I neither *see* nor *feel* the energy as much as I feel guided from the High Self to work in an area. This approach is very common with healers and comes easily with practice. As always, faith, intention, and the belief in a Higher Power are the only prerequisites for you to start.

The Healer's Responsibility

Healers have a tremendous responsibility when they enter another's energy field. A person coming to another and asking for healing is extremely vulnerable. Their defenses are down. Not only are they needy, but in the process of becoming receptive to another's energy, they are also extremely sensitive to the energy around them.

This vulnerability is not limited to just the energy coming in through the hands, but to the healer's overall energy field, and most importantly, each and every word spoken. Have you ever noticed how the decor and atmosphere varies in one doctor's office or another? Have you ever refused to return to a certain practitioner because of the *vibe* of the office environment, or the tone of voice of the receptionist? Healing starts with common courtesy and a pleasant environment. Anything less deprives the healer and the client of the full healing potential that is available.

This is a very general overview of hands-on healing. There are many techniques and modalities taught, all of which have value. There is much material and classes are available in methods such as Reiki, polarity therapy, Tai Na, etc. In the next chapter we'll look at one specific approach, Chironic Healing, which has proven very successful for me personally. Let's first look at some more avenues for healing.

Absent Healing

Healing does not always require you to be present physically with the client. Tremendous work can be accomplished at a distance, as in *absent healing*. In theory, anything that we can do to heal a person in our presence can be accomplished equally as well when we are at a distance from the client, because we can cross the barriers of time and space when working with a person's energy field. Absent healing involves mental imagery along with intention—combined with love, this process is not confined to time and space.

The experience and process of absent healing is extremely powerful. It not only provides one of the greatest services that one human being can offer another, but it opens the doors to more of the subtle, spiritual nature that lies within us. Some of my most profound spiritual experiences have occurred as a result of the process of absent healing.

The reason is that this process, as opposed to the hands-on method, requires one to go within and focus on mental and spiritual levels. This requires a little more concentration, at least in the beginning phase, but the personal payoff for both the healer and the one being healed is tremendous. In a sense it gives us a more intense focus because there is nothing on the physical level to distract us.

Absent healing is proof beyond any doubt that we have the ability to cross the limiting parameters of time and space. On many occasions I have worked with someone who was at a distance from me, only to later receive a phone call of confirmation. Usually it was something like, "Were you sending me light or something last night? I feel great!" or, " I don't know what you did, but I certainly feel better now." This obviously provides us great joy and satisfaction. However, *never forget to credit Source for all of your success.*

This type of healing also asks of us not to be limited in our thinking, nor deny what is possible in the healing arena. Let me share with you one personal example of this.

A few years back a dear friend in Florida telephoned me to ask my help in performing absent healing on another friend, also in Florida. Three of us, one in Florida, one in Illinois, and one in Colorado decided to perform an absent healing in unison. The issue was this: the woman asking for healing had been diagnosed with a large brain tumor. Her doctors had reviewed the situation thoroughly and had concluded that the only solution was to perform exploratory surgery on her brain.

We coordinated our healing session so as to be able to heal her simultaneously. Our first session was about one week prior to her scheduled surgery, while the second was two nights before the surgery. I had not received any feedback from our sessions until a couple of days after the second one. Not fully surprised, I was elated to receive a phone call from my friend that our client indeed had gone to the presurgery exam only to find that the tumor was practically nonexistent!

Most likely the patient awaiting surgery was more surprised than we were. *Surgery was not required*—more proof in the power of spiritual healing and going beyond the limitations of time and space!

To be successful in this form of work, it helps greatly if the healer has accomplished to some degree the ability to concentrate. Concentration helps greatly because when you are working with someone not present physically, you will need to stay in the individual's energy field for a minimum length of time, say ten to twenty minutes.

It is also important, as in all forms of healing, that you always ask Source and the Soul of the individual if you can be a channel for healing. In rare cases, you will not be allowed to perform any healing work. You must always be sensitive to this possibility. After you ask, the energy and feeling should flow easily when you call the person's name. If not, then stop immediately, give thanks, and do not pursue any healing at that time. There are situations we may not fully understand in which the Soul has chosen to take on a specific ailment for a certain length of time. Until the Soul has decided the lesson or experience has been fulfilled, deep healing of that ailment is not allowed. If you attempt to perform any type of in-depth work in such a situation, you will feel blocked, or unable to get the energy flowing.

There are many approaches to absent healing, just as there are many modalities in healing others at the physical level. *Never limit yourself as to what can be accomplished at a distance.* Whatever modality you find successful in healing others while in their presence can be applied during absent healing. Again, we're working with energy, not substance. In absent healing we're bringing an individual energy pattern to us, correcting it, then sending it back to the individual in the physical realm. We take ourselves out of time and space, correct and return the pattern, and then bring ourselves back to time and space.

The process is very simple. Start by simply drawing an individual to you mentally. Surround them in pure light energy and ask for them to be healed at all levels. This is essentially the process in prayer circles. The process can be more complex, such as sending someone various colors, balancing chakras, performing etheric surgery, performing etheric acupuncture, Reiki, or other methods.

Concentration is important, but more important is *intention*. Intention is the reason prayer works so well. Very few people who pray for another have any understanding of energy, nor do they work necessarily with healing energy at a conscious level. What they do have is *love and intention* for another—this is really all anyone needs to start healing others. *Love and intention* draws to the process tremendous Universal forces.

Here's a good protocol to start with.

Absent Healing Meditation

Get yourself calm and centered. As in all forms of meditation and healing, be certain you have a quiet, clear space without interruptions for as long as you need it. Ask Source for you to be a healing channel for the person you desire: "I ask to be a healing channel for (name) at this time." As you call the person's name, count to ten and bring the person's image in front of you. At this point, be very sensitive to your own energy level and flow. If you feel as if the energy is dropping, or a sensation of feeling blocked as if something were not right, simply give thanks and move on. There are some situations that do not allow you to perform any type of healing—the Soul must continue to go through the current experience.

Once you know you have the "okay," draw the person to you, see him or her surrounded in pure white light energy. See them joyous and happy. Even if you know the exact details of the problem, choose to only energize the positive, perfect condition. Hold your hands out and imagine that the person to be healed is suspended just in front of you physically. Work your healing energy as if they were in reality just in front of you. If you are not able to see or visualize the person, simply concentrate on their name, or feel them in your presence.

Perform whatever modality works best for you. Bring in color, perform chakra balancing, remove blockages, insert etheric acupuncture needles, or whatever you would do if the person were physically there. Work at least for five minutes, but never more than twenty minutes.

With a little practice in this arena, you will find that you will develop the ability to see and feel clearly the areas that need healing.

At some point in your session visualize your friend completely happy, healed, and joyful. See the light of his or her Soul descend and fill up their entire body. Surround them in love and ask that the healing energy of the Christ descend upon them.

When you feel your work is complete, send the pattern you have just healed back. Count backward, ten to one, and ask that the pattern be sent back to the person and that perfect health is restored. See and feel their energy leave you. Know that you have performed a great service to that soul.

Absent healing with a number of people in a group setting is tremendously powerful. Remember that the power of group energy is proportionate to the square of the number of people, not the total number of people present. The keys to groups are the same: *intention and love.* The other element, which is important, is *focus.* Once the group is focused, either through prayer or meditation, have those present bring forth verbally the names of those in need. It is important to allow at least a few seconds with each soul, and not rush through a list of names. This allows time for the healing energy to focus, build, and then be sent to the person for healing.

Healing an Area

We've been focusing our attention on healing individuals, but healing a geographical area is also extremely powerful and beneficial. There are two primary facets in this type of healing work. One is to heal and uplift everyone in that area, while the other is to help all of the Earth elements in the area, such as balancing natural disasters, or for general healing of the energy patterns of the planet in a specific area. However, no matter what your focus is, healing energy sent to an area uplifts, heals, and transmutes everything (living or inanimate) in the area to a certain degree.

An example of this would be sending healing energy to an area that just suffered a natural disaster, such as flooding, a volcano, earthquake, etc. When you are healing this area, either individually or through a group, you are helping those who have just suffered, and you are balancing the energies of Earth in that area so that future events of this type

Healing an area of Earth heals the individuals, as well as all life forms in that area. Mother Earth receives healing and responds to the Healer with healing and nurturing to the healer.

will be less intense. Mother Earth is an entity not totally unlike we humans. She is vast and much more complex than us, but a living organism nevertheless. When we send healing energy to Her, She responds like we do. She feels the nurturing and the love. Her energy field is repaired, and negativity gets transmuted. She receives the healing consciously and returns healing and love to the source of the healing—to us.

As in all forms of healing, we are nearly unlimited in what we can perform and accomplish. When we are based in Love, we can assist the healing process for vast areas of Earth, and we can help transmute pockets of negative energy, which have accumulated over time (energized by humans!). Mother Earth will respond to our love. She will return this love energy to us—we just need to be more sensitive to it.

At the time of this writing, many natural disasters around the globe are occurring. Weather patterns are changing drastically, as well. Sending healing energy to specific areas may not totally prevent these greater events, but it will help balance them and protect those in the region. What can happen is that healing an area will transmute the negative human energetics that have built up over time, resulting in less cataclysmic events.

Humans tend to feed on the energy in their environment. Consequently, healing an area heals the energy of that environment. People in that area are healed from this type of work directly, as well as healed from the newer, clearer energy in their environment.

As in absent healing, this type of healing process can be accomplished either individually or as a group. Groups are extremely powerful in this regard—we'll look more closely at group energy below.

To heal a specific area, simply ask Source that you be a channel for healing for (area). Examples: Phoenix, Baghdad,

Thailand, planet Earth, your apartment complex, etc. Bring in the image of the area you wish to heal and hold pure white light around and through it for five to ten minutes. Ask that all living beings in that area receive healing, balance, and uplift. Ask that Mother Earth be healed as well.

Remember the keys of *intention and love*. The more concentration abilities you have, the more focus you can provide. Once you are proficient in working with healing areas, you can begin to send an area a specific color, or anchor a violet flame of transmutation there, or even send a specific quality of energy, such as love, or wisdom, or discernment, or peace to the area.

An example of this would be to focus on an area such as the Mideast, and bring in the all-encompassing white light. Ask to be a channel for peace and understanding. It is important that you try and not bring in your personal opinions or feelings; otherwise do not work with this area. The people of certain areas need wisdom and understanding, because they are in an environment that energizes fear, paranoia, and war. Healing these areas with the healing qualities mentioned will help these people receive wisdom, and will help transmute their environment so that their soul food will be purified, even if in extremely subtle ways.

One particular meditation I use for a local area is especially powerful. Not only does it send waves of light to the area, but it also serves to uplift and expand tremendously the one meditating. It goes as follows:

Light Energy Meditation

Get yourself calm and focused. After you are confident that you are centered and can hold that space for at least ten minutes, see around you a cylinder of pure light energy. This cylinder should start out to be about three feet in radius in all directions. This sounds simple, but it may take a few sessions to be able to visualize this field omnidirectionally and hold it. As you hold this cylinder of light around you, see and feel it to be anchored deep within the Earth below you, and extending infinitely above you.

Once you can maintain this field, hold in your consciousness the intention of healing, uplift, and transmutation. Know that whatever and whoever comes in contact with this field will feel and experience these attributes. As always, ask Source to be a channel for healing and upliftment.

After you have held this field for a few moments, allow yourself to relax at a deeper level, and immerse yourself in this beautiful field of light.

Become the Light.

As you physically and mentally relax further, you will become weightless and vibrant. As you become this energy (feel at one with it), slowly see this field extending outward in all directions to include the house or structure where you live. Hold that field for one minute. Spread this field again outwardly to include the neighborhood in which you live, holding it for a few moments. Know that all the while you are healing and uplifting all of the life forms within your cylinder and that Source is working through you, aiding and uplifting you as well.

Finally, extend your cylinder to include the city and/or state in which you live. See the light field spread throughout this vast region, keeping in focus that you are at the center of this wonderful vortex.

You are the cocreator of a magnificent healing process for many souls! Eventually you can extend this field to embrace the entire planet.

You should now feel totally weightless and vibrant. You are out of your three-dimensional body, and may possibly reach what some call the fifth or sixth dimensions.

This is a simple exercise, but it takes some practice to hold the energy for any length of time. The reward of deep peace and joy are well worth your efforts!

Groups

Extremely powerful healing can take place when many people meditate or pray together in a group with the same intent. In chapter I we discussed the power of numbers when individuals gather together with the same intent; the power is proportionate to the square of the number of individuals involved.

Groups tend to become more powerful over time, due to the length of time it takes for individuals to get accustomed to each other, as well as the time needed for solidifying the techniques they employ. This applies to all group settings, not just healing groups: management meetings, school classes, social groups, etc.

All the techniques and concepts in healing others that we discussed previously in the book apply to group healing as well. The main difference is that we have increased the power of the group (which, by the way, tends to attract more of the spiritual kingdom for assistance). It is important for one or more persons in the group to verbalize the process throughout the session, providing focus and intent. This doesn't necessarily mean that a group needs a leader, but a group of this nature needs to maintain focus. To keep this, one individual must be the leader, at least for a particular session.

I personally like having the group arranged in a circle. This helps focus all of the energy, especially when absent healing is performed. Also, it helps if there is a standard procedure, or protocol, that is basically the same each week. Too much change and variation and the intent can get lost, with the energy getting scattered.

Groups are like individuals in that they tend to have a personality and a soul. They tend to evolve, much like individuals. However, the group's general purpose and intent should always remain the same.

The following is an example of a very effective group-healing meditation. These meditations tend to last a little longer than an individual meditation because of the time required to get everyone focused, and also because of the depth and power that is available. This meditation is for healing both the individuals present and for those in need at a distance. It has been written in the first person.

Group Healing Meditation

We call forth the Light of Protection to surround this room and those present in this healing work. We ask to be channels for Source in healing ourselves and others who are in need. We call forth only those energies and entities which work with the forces of the white light to assist and guide us as necessary.

Visualize a root system extending from the bottoms of your feet deep into the Earth. Feel the Earth and feel the grounding of your energy. Allow all of your scattered energies to be grounded through this root system. (The leader is silent for a minute.)

Now visualize a ball of radiant white light suspended about eight inches over the top of your head.

Imagine that from this ball of light a thread of the light energy is extending down through the top of your head. The energy of light begins to fill your entire body, from head to toe. See and feel this energy flow through your head, shoulders, arms, back, chest, solar plexus, lower abdomen, hips, legs, ankles, and out through the feet to the Earth. As the light flows in, know that it is rejuvenating, uplifting, and revitalizing each and every cell of your body. In the light you are renewed. The light will uplift and heal all of our selves: physical, emotional, and mental. Hold this image for a few moments; you are a channel of light energy as it flows from your Soul to the Earth, healing, cleansing, and transmuting. Allow yourself to feel this for a moment. (Leader is silent for a few minutes.)

From this same ball of radiant white light, imagine a stream of green healing and grounding energy flowing into the top of your head. Know that green balances and heals. It helps us to integrate our fragmented selves. For a moment imagine that you are standing in a glass cylinder. Slowly this cylinder is filling up with this green, vitalizing energy of healing. You are totally immersed in this green energy. Every cell in your body is being washed with this healing energy. (Hold this energy for a few minutes.)

(Note: if your group is relaxed and disciplined enough to continue, then do so with the following as a suggested method. If not, gently come out of the meditation—good job!)

At this time if any of you present wish to bring forth someone's name(s) who is in need of healing, please do so. We will hold that being in light for a few moments. (Allow names to be brought forward verbally. When the process is complete, give thanks for healing to occur in those souls' lives.)

(Note: if your group is focused and open, now would be a good time to send healing energy to an area of Earth in need. If not, again, gently bring the group back to the physical, giving thanks for the good work that's been done, and to Source.)

We ask at this time to be healing channels for the area of (city, country, Earth, etc.). *We send light to* (same). *We know this light will help heal and bring peace to all of those in this region. We ask that all negative energies be transmuted, so that Earth can move on with her natural flow of evolution.*

Hold this energy for this area for at least two to three minutes, depending on the experience and discipline of your group. After this latter process is complete, slowly bring the group back to present time and space. Be sure to come back slowly. You will find that all present will feel very relaxed, at peace, and vibrant!

Advanced Techniques

Before we look at a specific, very effective school of healing, Chironic Healing, let's examine some of the more advanced processes and techniques available to you as a healer. Tremendous healing can take place simply by opening your heart and allowing Source to do the work through you. Naturally, practice, knowledge, and experience help greatly, but in the end we are simply channels for the Source of All to help others along their way.

In this process you will find some who are not ready to receive healing, and others who believe they are ready, but have not learned the appropriate lesson, and therefore the healing energies will be blocked for you. As you practice and expand in the healing arena, you will stumble upon some very profound experiences and techniques. Be open and always give credit to Source.

As far as advanced techniques are concerned, remember that we are essentially energy, manifest as dense, physical bodies. When we can learn to manipulate energy somewhat and realign another's energy pattern, it may appear as a miracle that the person is suddenly *healed*. From the vantage point of the energy pattern, this is no miracle at all—it is simply the resetting of the original pattern around the individual, allowing the body to heal itself. This realignment occurs with the agreement of the individual's Soul, and is empowered by both your Soul and theirs. This is the magic that occurs as a manifestation of Divine Love between two Souls, and when an individual is consciously using his or her mind positively to invoke self-healing, the healing process is accelerated greatly.

Blockages

Blockages in our energy pattern are eventually reflected as disease and/or pain in our physical body. A blockage is the most common challenge a healer faces. Most of the time you can detect a blockage by scanning the pattern with your hands—the blocked area will usually feel much warmer than the rest of the pattern. With practice, locating a major blockage in the energy field will become quite easy. Your own intuition will usually guide you to the exact area that needs work. Also, remember common sense—a few questions directed to your patient will often give you all the information you need.

One way to release the blockage is to hold your hands perpendicular to the body and walk through the whole pattern, head to foot. Imagine yourself *shoveling* out any unwanted energy. As you do this, ask Source to "release all blockages that are no longer for this Soul's higher good." After this process, flick your hands to clear them of any unwanted energy. Visualize any energy not your own going into the light, or simply ask that it go into the light. Immediately after this bring in pure white-light energy to the pattern, or specifically to an area where a blockage was removed. This must be done, because if an object (blockage) is removed, a void is temporarily created and the energy must be replaced.

Another way to remove a blockage is to simply pull it out. This requires extreme caution so that you do not disturb the portion of the individual's pattern that is in good shape, and do not pick up any pattern and/or energy that would attach to your energy field. This technique could actually be termed *psychic surgery*, which is much more specific in removing or healing a blockage.

Once you know where the blockage is that you want to remove, place your hands there. *It is absolutely necessary that you have protected the area, yourself, and your client with the white Light of Protection prior to this work. You must also surround yourself and your client with the silver bubble.* You have two main choices at this point:

◆ Visualize the negative or unwanted energy blockage magnetically going to your hands, like a magnet. Watch and feel as the energy comes into your palms. Immediately throw this energy into the light (it helps to visualize the light somewhere at a distance below the feet). Immediately place the palms back on the area and visualize green healing energy replacing that which you just removed.

◆ Or simply ask Source to pull out any unwanted energy and place in your hands. Perform all of the same steps as above and replace this energy with green, healing energy. Always be sure to send any unwanted energies to the light.

When you sense an area of the body is cold, it usually means that there is a lack of energy in that area or a major lesson has been taken on by the Soul of the individual. Sometimes, you'll find that no amount of healing to this area will be effective. It is totally acceptable to go ahead with the healing of that particular area, keeping in mind that if you are blocked then you must pull away, leaving Source to allow the Soul to work out its plan. Perhaps the individual simply needs the area energized. In this case, place one hand over the area and start moving it in circles, asking Source to bring the proper energy to the area.

However, at other times in a similar situation, your energy flow may become quite strong. In those cases it may be that the individual has an immense build-up of blocked matter that needs to be removed. In other words, it's a type of blockage that requires even more work than previously discussed. Simply place your hands in the area, ask Source to assist you in removing "all elements that are no longer for the highest good of the individual," and then *flick* off the energy into the light, as outlined above. Repeat this procedure as many times as required, until you are confident the many layers are removed.

Always consciously send unwanted energy into the light— never just flick it in the air, since it may hang around and cling to someone else, including yourself! Your intention will send it to Source. Also, be sure to bring in white light or green to replace the energy you just removed. It is extremely important in this technique to never work when you are tired. There are many unwanted energies ready to attack you.

Clairvoyant Sight

Many healers while doing their work see clairvoyantly the various colors, patterns, and blockages in the human energy field. This is seeing with the *inner eye*, not through visual sight with the eyes. We all have this ability to a greater or lesser degree, and some have simply refined the ability and use it to better understand where and how to heal someone. The development of this ability is not at all required, nor is it a prerequisite to be successful in hands-on healing. This same process is what many psychics use to read a person's past and future. A clear psychic is simply reading the energy pattern of their client at the very subtle levels.

If you practice any form of healing over a length of time you will no doubt begin to see or feel energy in one form or another in ways that are new to you. This is normal. Do not judge it, but simply acknowledge your experience. You can choose to utilize these newer abilities or simply acknowledge them and work in traditional ways, which you may feel more comfortable with.

A good example of how this type of *seeing* can assist you is when you are sitting at the head of your client's table, and you sense or *see* a blockage in the energy pattern. Many times this can be seen as a brown energy pattern, for example, in the spinal column. With your hands over the client's head, send a strong flow of bright, white energy *flushing energy* down the spinal column. Follow this with a flow of green, healing energy. Ask Source to assist you in removing and transmuting all blockages in that area. You may want to work your hands directly now in the area as mentioned in the previous paragraphs to *pull out* any unwanted energy.

One of the most difficult tasks as you evolve in your healing work is to not judge what you see or feel as you work, but just observe your experience. Use these detections as a type of advanced diagnosis, which your High Self is providing you to better help your client.

Visualization

In Chapter III we discussed at some length the power of visualizing the perfect body part to enhance self-healing and help manifest health. This same technique and philosophy can be used on another who needs a body part energized, although the client must eventually be the one performing the visualization in order for the process to be truly effective.

One of the keys in this technique is to *never place any mental imagery or thought energy on the diseased or malfunctioning condition.* You may see the diseased area with your inner eye, but only acknowledge it—do not spend any time on it.

When you put energy into the problematic area, not only are you limiting your own positive, uplifting energy for your client, but also your client may unconsciously feel this and the healing process will consequently be hampered. The ultimate bad example is a massage therapist who works on you and constantly tells you how tight, how stiff, and how bad your condition is. Instead of leaving the session relaxed and rejuvenated, you will probably leave uptight, tense, and worried about your health! Remember that individuals under your care are extremely vulnerable, and they will pick up your feelings and thoughts more readily since their defenses are diminished. *You are the therapist—it is imperative that you do not emphasize the negative conditions!*

> *Only energize the perfect condition. Never put mental energy into the imperfect condition.*

While working in an area in which you know the body is damaged, simply stop for a few moments and hold the thought form of the perfect body part. See it manifesting in the body, and see it in pure, white light essence. At very deep levels you are also assisting your client to set up this exact thought form in their subconscious mind. If your client is receptive, you should mention to him or her the power of thought and visualization. In the end, his or her High Self will become the healer.

If you are not a *visual* type person and know that a specific area of the body is damaged, simply ask Source to assist you. Place your hands over the area to be healed, ask Source for guidance and to manifest the perfect bodily part, then hold pure white light essence in that area. You are now a channel for the perfect condition.

Another way to use the mind in healing another is to open the acupuncture meridians with your mind and fingertips. Simply ask Source to open up these critical energy currents and trace the lines (meridians) with your forefingers, while visualizing the perfect flow of energy with your mind. Ask Source to assist you in the proper direction of this flow for each meridian. In essence, what you can conceive in your thoughts, you can manifest in the healing arena. Obviously, your healing will be enhanced in this area if you have a basic understanding of acupuncture and the directions of the body's meridians.

Violet Flame

In Chapter III we looked at color and discussed the principles and qualities of the energy of violet. The action and process described in the meditation in that chapter can be applied to another individual. I personally have applied it in a couple of ways with some very good success.

One is to mentally invoke the violet flame and direct it to a specific area of the body that is in need of tremendous healing—say, for example, a bleeding ulcer, or a broken bone. *This does not replace professional care and experienced doctors! Our energy work on serious ailments comes after the specialists have stopped the bleeding, and examined the bones!* However, what the violet flame can do is assist in transmuting those blockages and distortions in the energy pattern that helped cause the problem to begin with.

The violet flame works on many levels, not just physical or emotional. Of course, when working with problems like those just mentioned, it is good to apply all of your known techniques to reestablish the various levels in the individual's pattern—physical, mental, emotional, and even spiritual. I also end each session by invoking the violet frame around the individual, asking Source to transmute all of the elements at any level that no longer serves the patient in his or her life.

Another scenario in which the violet flame is useful is those times of travel when you are sleeping in a new space. For example, before I sleep in a different bed, especially in a hotel, I always clear the space, invoke a field of white light energy, protect it, and anchor the violet flame in and around the bed. This insures protection against unwanted energies and transmutes any and all negative or heavy energies that may be lurking in the bed or the room.

The following can be applied in seconds and can clear and protect you in a new room. Apply this in a form of meditation, either sitting or lying on your back just before falling asleep.

Sleep Protection Meditation

Ask Source to assist you in clearing and protecting your sleeping space. Begin first by visualizing a swirling vortex of white light moving out all negative or unwanted energies (clearing). Lighting a candle is helpful also. Then visualize the ceiling, floor, and all four walls becoming a shield of white light. Call forth the white light of protection to assist you in this procedure. With the areas sealed, begin to fill the room with a warm, radiant, pure white light. Feel this process occur, as if someone were pouring a liquid light into a container, then capping it. Finally, invoke and visualize the violet flame (see Chapter III) engulfing and surrounding the bed you are about to sleep on. Now enjoy a good night's sleep!

Apply this quick technique, and you'll sleep better and wake up feeling more like you have slept in your own bed. This little technique will not only clear and protect the room; it will actually bring the vibrations closer to yours. The result is that you won't feel as heavy or drained upon awakening. You have also uplifted the room, and prepared it for the next person, as well.

In all forms and techniques in healing, Source knows all. The one to be healed knows as well, at least at the level of his or her High Self. By always asking Source to be a channel, no matter how accomplished or how much of a beginner you are, you will always be doing the proper work on the individual.

Energy exchanges during healing sessions occur sometimes at very deep levels—levels far beyond our waking, conscious mind. Source will direct these energies for us, once we have set our heart and our intentions in motion. Remember that service is a natural process for our Soul, and healing another is one of the greatest services one can provide! *Source will always be with you in your healing journeys!*

V

Chironic
Healing

In nearly all known cultures of man, there have been traces or full proof of the practice of natural healing in one form or another. From the stories of ancient Atlantis to the more current remedies of the American Indian and the shamans, natural healing has always played a large role in human life. Though many modalities have proven to be successful, there appears to be no one single modality of healing that is a cure-all for everyone, all of the time. Nearly all techniques work to some extent, and different individuals respond differently to different types of healing. One constant thread that runs through the modalities that are successful is the openness and faith of the client toward the technique. When the patient believes he or she will be healed, or at least will improve, the chances for success are much greater.

Furthermore, as one's consciousness and state of health changes, the type of treatment changes, or at least needs to be adjusted, because the *body consciousness* has changed. The vibrations and frequencies of the body energetics have changed. What was at one time an effective modality may no longer have the same effect. This is the reason it is so important to investigate and explore various avenues of healing when one is experiencing a chronic or difficult problem or challenge.

One relatively new, yet extremely powerful, form of hands-on healing is *Chironic Healing*. The title comes from the name *Chiron*, a great and powerful healer of the spiritual realms. Dr. Trevor Creed introduced Chironic Healing in Australia a few years ago. He relinquished a very successful practice as a chiropractor of twenty-five years after realizing the power and long-term benefits of Chironic Healing. He has since maintained quite a large practice in southeast Australia, and has traveled around the world teaching the principles of Chironic Healing.

Principles of Chiron

The Chironic Healing methods involve using the hands and mind to heal another person by realigning their body's perfect *template*. This takes place primarily at the etheric level but, as always, healing energy spans the various levels of the human energy field, healing and balancing throughout the subtle layers. This form of hands on healing is spiritually based, and follows the premise and belief in the *One Creative Intelligence* in the Universe, which regulates all functions and all motion in our physical existence.

The basic balancing and realignment of the body's etheric counterpart is performed by the mind and the hands, and takes place primarily through geometric shapes in the body's energy field: diamonds, triangles, and lines. When these shapes are realigned and reconfigured, the body has a greater opportunity to heal itself and maximize its quota of energy.

The focus in this chapter will be to discuss some of the basics of Chironic Healing, how to apply them, and the unlimited potential of Chironic Healing in helping to alleviate pain and human suffering. For reference, the primary book for this subject is *The Healing Principles of Chiron* (by Andrew and Trevor Creed), listed in Appendix II, which provides much more detail in terms of understanding the various etheric layers of our energy field, the use of color and sound, lines of energy, etc.

One great advantage which I have personally found in the philosophy of Chironic Healing is the openness and creative potential that it offers. There are no limits in healing, as long as one is willing to be open, creative, and use the unlimited potentials of the mind to visualize the results desired. In other words, if you can visualize or feel a certain positive outcome, it can become a reality.

One personal example of this visualization is when working over a client who has a physical blockage, if I feel strongly that he or she would benefit from acupuncture, I visualize myself inserting etheric needles, one by one, into the various locations along the meridians. I always ask Source to continue the healing process for the appropriate length of time. Remember that the etheric is the subtle energy field around our physical body that actually allows the energy to flow and be processed, eventually healing the physical body. Your healing potential is only limited by your mind and your faith.

Another excellent approach in Chironic Healing is that it takes the mystery out of psychic surgery, making it both simple and practical. Psychic surgery is no more than repairing the etheric levels by removing, replacing, or weaving parts of it with the proper lines of force. The etheric template is the counterpart of the physical body, and any healing or repair work done at the etheric level is eventually reflected as health at the physical level. We'll look more closely at psychic surgery at the close of the chapter.

Most hands-on healing techniques call for positioning your hands in an open fashion so that healing energy can flow through your palms into the client's body. Chironic Healing allows this also, but more importantly outlines specific lines of force which can be repaired and reconfigured. Most of the procedures of this technique in Chironic Healing consist primarily of realigning the pattern with the forefingers of each hand.

Figure 5 is the top view of what is termed the "top diamond." This geometric configuration is one of the major focal points for Chironic Healing. The diamond has focal points and centers which represent every major portion of our body, including organs, extremities, etc., much like reflexology has points in the feet and hands. By balancing these points and others, healing and balance can occur in the body.

This diamond is more accurately represented when you envision it as three-dimensional, with height, width, and depth. It is located just above the head, with another similar diamond located just below the feet. There are front and back diamonds as well. Chironic Healing has many steps, facets, and possibilities, but it is most powerful if you balance the top diamond first, and after your work is complete, rebalance it as a final step.

Realigning the Major Shapes

Perhaps the best way to describe some of the techniques in Chironic Healing is to walk through, step by step, the major areas of the etheric pattern. Always start with the client lying face down. Assuming you have cleared and protected the area (see previous chapter), stand over the person and surround him or her in a glowing white bubble of light. Also surround yourself in this bubble. The white light is the great healer and connects you to Source and the highest frequencies available in which to heal. It is literally a requirement to successful healing.

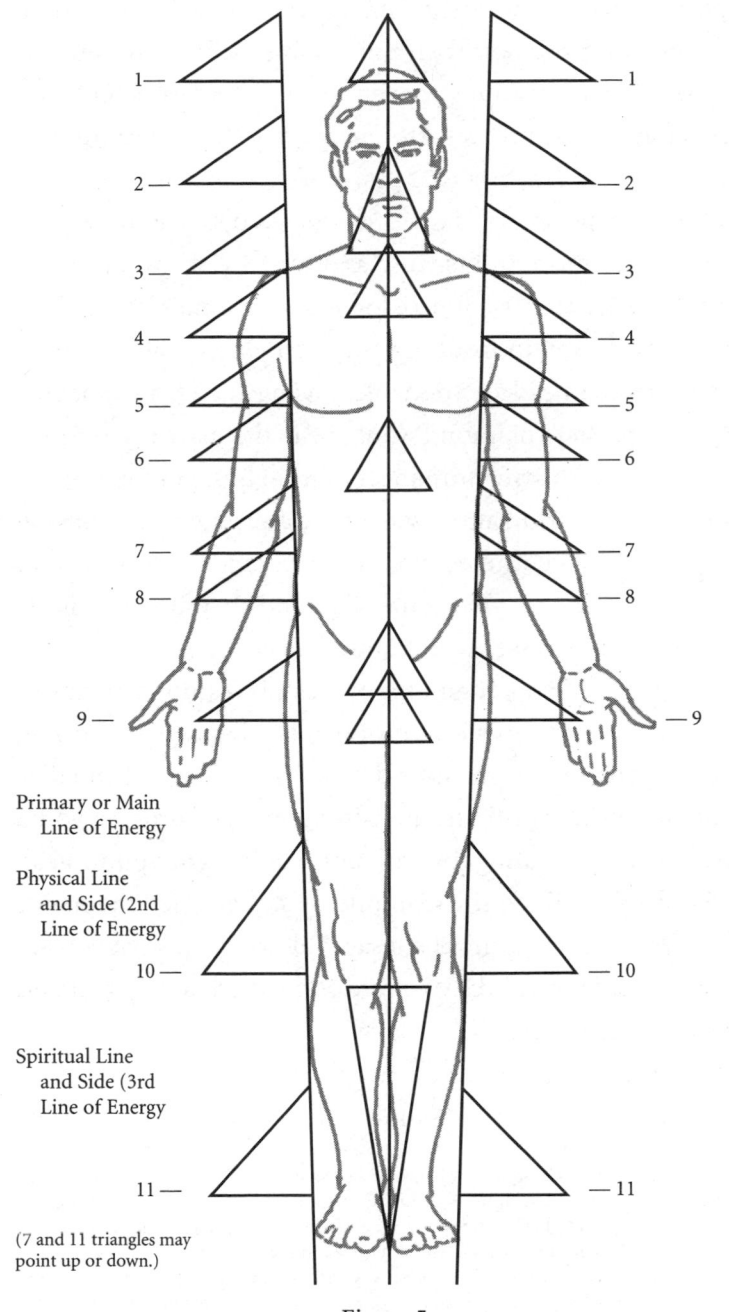

Primary or Main
Line of Energy

Physical Line
and Side (2nd
Line of Energy

Spiritual Line
and Side (3rd
Line of Energy

(7 and 11 triangles may
point up or down.)

Figure 5
The Etheric Lines and Triangles (common locations).

(This drawing based on illustration © Chironic Enterprises 1990)

Next, surround the client with a silver bubble of protection. Also surround yourself with this bubble. It protects you and the client from unwanted frequencies, and it acts as a filter and a healer as well. It protects the energy field from harmful frequencies, while drawing to it powerful healing energies. Silver can also help repair damaged tissue, dissolve unwanted growths, and flush and cleanse a group of cells of unwanted viruses or bacteria. Ask Source for you to be a clear channel for healing the person in front of you. You are now ready to heal.

Walk to the head of the table. Facing the client, imagine where the person's diamond would be in the space just over his or her head. Run your forefingers through the outline of the diamond, visualizing at the same time a silver essence flowing smoothly through these lines. With practice you will soon begin to see or feel where the diamond may be broken, or where more silver essence is required. *Remember that intention is the key*. Even if you do not see or feel this diamond, or any of the lines of the energy pattern, you are realigning and healing through your intention. Your detailed knowledge of the diamond and other configurations in the pattern provide you a better focus for healing, but are not required for you to heal. Often I have outlined the diamond or straightened the major lines of force and had my client say, "I don't know what you are doing, but it feels good." We are working with a very real and powerful energy here.

To heal through specific areas of the etheric diamond (Figure 6, insert), use your intuition or a form of muscle testing*

---

* Muscle testing is a technique that helps the healer get a "yes" or "no" answer, and can take a variety of forms. A popular technique is for the client to lie face up, straighten one arm and point it upward, resisting the healer's pressure. The healer will try to push to arm down, while silently asking a question such as, "Should I perform a certain technique on this person?" A "yes" answer is indicated by a strong resistance, and a "no" answer by less or little resistance. One way to start this technique is to silently ask the patient what his or her name is. Obviously, the real name should provide the healer with strong resistance, while a fake name would afford little or no resistance.

to determine which of the thirty-seven points need healing. Additionally, your client has probably already indicated to you the major reason he or she is requesting healing. If you are able to determine these specific points, imagine a silver needle of *energy essence* being inserted into that point. To do this, place one needle there with your forefinger as you do this mentally. At the same time place one on the opposite side to maintain balance. For example if you know that liver, pt. #18, needs balance, place a needle there and one at #19 exactly opposite (refer to Figure 6). *It's important that your hands, your heart, and your mind are working together.* Your mind is asking and visualizing the needles, your heart is open to the flow of energy, and your hands are directing and placing the energy in the diamond.

If you are unable to determine the specific points, simply point your forefingers into the diamond, relax your mind, and ask Source to heal through you. You will feel the energy flow through your fingertips. As you allow and relax, you'll find that your fingers may rotate a little, which is actually Source assisting you in rotating the diamond back to its proper alignment. Once you know you have completed this stage, place silver essence needles in each of the four corners of the diamond.

The final step is balancing the diamond. Place your hands, palms up, in a cupped position under the diamond and feel the energy. Many times one side will actually feel heavier than the other. Subtly balance out this energy, similar to the way you played with a Slinky as a kid, until the energy feels balanced on both sides. You are now finished with the diamond. Many times you may want to go back and rebalance at the end of your session, especially if you have performed some major work on the pattern.

Next, balance the diamond just below the feet. This is a much quicker step: simply outline the diamond with silver essence, place needles at the four corners, and balance with palms up and cupped.

You can perform the various Chironic Healing steps in any order. However, by balancing the diamond first, the remaining work goes much easier, and tends to *hold* for a longer period of time.

The next step I like to perform is balancing and extending the *lines of force* (refer to Figure 6, color insert). As you can see there are three major lines of energy, which run longitudinally with the body. These lines are responsible for much of our vitality and physical strength and tend to get compressed, broken, or *blocked* through stress and any number of blockages. When this happens, your overall energy level is diminished.

With the patient still face down (prone), stand at their side. With hands together, palm to palm and forefingers pointed toward the lower back area, visualize the central line of energy, which extends just over the spine from below the feet to far above the head. Begin to open your arms with the hands and fingers following this central line of energy. As you do this, imagine that you are bringing in silver essence and realigning this line of force. You may see or feel this line. After some practice you will be able to determine where the line is broken, or compressed, or even jammed up.

In cases where the line shows any of these symptoms, they will require some stretching. To pull or stretch the line out, place the hands together, but curl the hands inwardly, with fingers back-to-back. From this position, pull and stretch the line out. In both of these moves, always return the hands to the original starting position near the mid- to lower-back area before pulling back out. With practice you will be able to stretch the lines and feel a smooth, continuous flow of energy. The line is complete. Simply repeat these steps for the right and left lines of the sides.

The third major geometric shape we want to realign in the field turns out to be a series of triangles. There are seven major triangles that correspond very roughly to the seven major chakras. These are also shown in Figure 6. With your forefingers starting together, simply outline each of the seven, starting with number one at the top. As you work with each triangle, visualize in your mind each triangle filled with a silver essence, and each one bright and clearly defined. The base of each triangle is the most important leg to realign. As with the other shapes, you will eventually be able to see or feel any broken or damaged lines in the triangles.

The triangles have a wonderful philosophic representation as well. Each one represents a powerful principle in Chironic Healing, as outlined below. What is most interesting is that when you begin to see and feel broken triangles and refer to the principles, you will find that the lack of balance with the principle is nearly always reflected in the etheric counterpart of the triangle itself. The most common example of this is the second triangle: "Caring for Yourself." Many, many healers and sincere spiritual people have this second triangle out of balance or broken simply because they do not take enough time for themselves.

The Seven Principles of Chiron

1st Triangle   The first principle of Chiron is to care for others. Caring for others effectively opens the triangle to create the outgoing force necessary to enable us to channel the healing force for healing others.

2nd Triangle   The second principle of Chiron is to care for yourself. This allows the triangle to prepare for the intake of energy necessary for the physical and self-healing.

3rd Triangle   The third principle of Chiron is to sit in quiet contemplation of your lessons and debts, to learn without resentment what it is that you are here to achieve.

4th Triangle   The fourth principle of Chiron is to give forth to the world all of the knowledge you have accumulated. This opens the caring level for those who are captive also in form (incarnate).

5th Triangle   The fifth principle of Chiron is to feel for others as you would feel for yourself. This is the conquential *feeling line* of the Master Diamond.

6th Triangle   The sixth principle is to stand tall on your journey and gather together your strength from the helping of others on your path.

7th Triangle   The seventh principle is to reach ever upward in your endeavor. So that what may seem a bogging down in the clay of life is actually a step in the direction of greater understanding.*

Balancing the Sacrum

Another simple, yet powerful step is to balance the sacrum (lower back). This step aids healing in all of the lower back area, especially at the sacrum and lumbar region.

With the client still face down, simply point the forefingers of each hand toward the sacrum and ask that the sacrum be balanced. Place the forefingers on either side of the client, just

---

* Derived from workshop materials distributed by Dr. Trevor Creed.

above the hips, pointing slightly downward and toward the sacrum. See light energy going to that area. Hold for a few seconds and know that the sacrum is indeed being balanced. It is that simple.

One other quick step I like to perform before turning the client face up is to move the hands through their field gently, while visualizing the color green flowing into them. Green is a very balancing and grounding color. Also, it is good to bring in a purple energy for the natural healing and balancing of the chakras. Chironic healing teaches us that the chakras can get blocked with *wedges,* through pollution, nuclear energy, and surrounding impure energies. Purple helps release these wedges.

Also, if there are any known areas of the back that need to be worked on, now is the time to do it. Place etheric needles where you need to, or if you prefer to place the hands directly on the patient for healing energy, feel free to do so at this point.

These are the basic steps in the prone position. Ask the client to now turn over, face up.

Mother Points

There are twenty-six "Mother Points" that correspond to twenty-six etheric levels of the basic pattern of our human energy field. There are a number of ways to check these points to see if balancing is required. Muscle testing is always an option if you feel competent with that technique. The following technique works quite well also.

Place the hands, palms down, just over the patient. Imagine that extending up and around your client are twenty-six levels of energy, much like the layers of onion skins on an onion. Slowly lift the hands away from the body, imagining that they pass through each individual level (layer). *Ask Source to balance each of the layers as you pass through them.* I also send balancing, green energy to each level. Each of these layers is very thin.

If you choose to be more specific with each point, there are detailed charts available* that will identify the exact representative area that is out of balance, as well as a specific color to use ot bring this area into balance. Knowledge of all the levels is not necessary—it is your intent that will balance these levels.

Solar Plexus Area

Perhaps the greatest area in our human condition that requires healing is the emotional/feeling center. Fortunately, Chironic Healing offers tremendous tools which assist this balancing process, without the client always needing to necessarily go through any type of emotional pain.

The solar plexus, the energy center extending forward from the navel area, is our feeling center in a number of ways. It is also a *vortex* of energy, and if one is not extremely careful, others can draw on this energy, depleting an individual of his or her own energy reserves. If we are out of control emotionally or our energy is already depleted and our defenses are down, the solar plexus can be severely damaged by intrusive energies that are always lurking around us. This is the reason you may feel drained after being in a large crowd—many people are unconsciously drawing on your energies.** Even in family situations and personal relationships, those you love dearly can unknowingly drain your energy reserves. Obviously this is not healthy.

The first step in working with another's solar plexus area, referred to in Chironic Healing as the *feeling pattern*, is to close down and restrict our connection to the outer world. To do

---

* These charts are contained in the primary text on Chironic Healing, *Principles in Chironic Healing*. See Appendix II.

** Again, the silver bubble is excellent protection against outside influences. The Light of Protection is very good as well in protecting the solar plexus area.

this, imagine that near the navel are a variety of small strands of energy extending upward. These are really frayed, or damaged, energy lines from the one central channel of the solar plexus. Take your hands, again palms down, one from each side of the solar plexus area, and pull them together as if you are pulling together all of the strands into one thread. Bring your hands completely together, and then open them slightly, leaving a space between them approximately the size of a quarter. This small area will allow the feeling pattern to stay connected to the outer world, but in a more limited fashion.

The solar plexus shouldn't be *wandering* around, so to speak, because at this level there are an infinite number of energies just waiting to tap into you. The solar plexus is a sensitive doorway and one must always be aware and guard this opening. Many of the intruding energies can throw you extremely off balance, drain your energy, and cause extreme irritability.

Next, you are going to release any or all of those individuals (entities) who are drawing on and attached to your client's energy field. The releasing of these energy drainers helps the client speed up their healing process, because he or she will be giving away less energy to others. Healing will take place even if you release these drainers for only a few moments. Most affected by these drainers are parents and others who have individuals that are very dependent on them emotionally. Substance abusers also have many leaks in their energy field.

Still standing near the patient's solar plexus area, imagine that your hand is a pair of scissors or a knife—whatever works for you. Move your hand through the imaginary field of lines (extending from the solar plexus region) that others have used to draw on your client's energy field, and imagine all of those lines being snipped by your scissors.

Immediately follow this action by turning your hands, palms down, and heal the snipped endings with the color green. Ask Source to help you heal these broken lines, placing your palms close to the client's solar plexus area. Hold this energy for a few seconds. Ask all of those who are now disconnected to draw upon their own source at this time. Remember that we all have free will, and an individual can choose to reconnect at any time.

Imagine now that there is a diamond shape, similar to the one above the head, which lies just over this same region. Trace this diamond with your fingers, again visualizing silver essence filling and making up this outline. Place a silver essence needle in each of the four corners, bringing balance and symmetry to the feeling center. Now, with palm down, place your right hand over this center. Your left hand will be extended, palm up, in a receptive posture. Ask Source to heal the feeling center, as you become a conduit for this energy flow. Assist this process by mentally bringing in the color purple to the feeling center and imagine that this center is the doorway for this purple energy to flow into the entire body. Hold that thought (energy flow) for a few moments. Just this one simple step of bringing in the purple essence provides tremendous healing to anyone.

Multiple Personalities

Another simple and quick Chironic technique helps the individual to get focused in the mental levels. In our modern world, we all tend to become mentally and emotionally scattered, sometimes functioning as a multitude of personalities. The human activities that are required to function upon our plane of existence stretch and stress the etheric patterns in and around the brain. This technique helps to bring our energy together in a *centered*, focused expression, while healing the etheric level.

Stand at the head of the table. Your client should still be face up, but it really doesn't matter. With arms straight and out-reached, palms facing together, mentally bring white light healing energy into your hands. Close your eyes and bring your palms together while asking Source to "balance the personalities." Repeat this a few times until your palms come together perfectly without any effort on your part. This is also a great tool for self-healing, and a great way to start your day. Simply perform this step while asking Source to balance your multiple personalities.

Balancing the TMJ

Another simple technique is excellent for the temporal-mandibular joint (TMJ) This joint is the primary structural point for talking and eating. When it is out of balance, it can reflect as pain in the jaw, headaches, clicking of the teeth, etc.

This technique utilizes the forefingers. Stand at the head of the table and place your forefingers at the main point in the jaw, pointing toward each other. Visualize white light emanating from your fingers. Pull the fingers back approximately one to two inches. Ask Source to balance the TMJ, and hold for five to ten seconds. Your work is done here. It is that simple.

It is helpful before sitting the client up, to once again balance the top diamond. Outline it with silver essence, place the silver needles at each of the four corners, and then with palms up balance the entire diamond from the bottom. At this point, ask your client to sit up slowly. Take your forefinger and *cross* over his or her forehead area in an "X" motion, asking Source to shut down any area (especially the third eye) that was opened unknowingly. Ask your client to stand slowly, and then walk around for a moment to be certain he or she is grounded.

These are just a few of the basic techniques of Chironic Healing. By employing these few steps, amazing healing and energy balancing will result. All of the aforementioned steps can also be used on yourself, as well as for those at a distance.

The Etheric, Perfect Pattern

In Chapter III we discussed many processes for healing yourself. Once your ability to concentrate is at a point that allows you to hold a pattern for at least five to ten minutes, you can bring your own etheric pattern to yourself by counting to ten, then performing all of the above steps on yourself.

As always, find a quiet place and ask Source to assist you in healing your own pattern. Remember that your pattern is weightless so you can rotate it, lift it, or move it in any way you want. Start by surrounding your pattern in a cocoon or bubble of white light. Then balance the diamond, stretch the lines, and clear the triangles—just as though it was someone else's pattern. Perform any/all procedures you feel appropriate. There is no hurry.

When you feel your work is complete, simply count backward, ten to one, and consciously send your pattern back to your body. This sounds somewhat bizarre, but it really does work, and many times you will begin to feel better in a matter of minutes or hours.

The same approach can be employed for healing those at a distance. The technique was covered in general in Chapter IV. Again, ask to be a healing channel for the person (mention the specific name), then count to ten and bring in his or her pattern. Once you have done this you can perform any type of healing technique(s) you wish. Start by going through the basic steps outlined above, and utilize any/all other healing steps you like. *Always send the pattern back.* Chironic Healing teaches us that if you do not send the pattern back (counting ten to one), the realigned and balanced pattern cannot heal the body. In other words, the effects of your healing work will not be fully manifest or reach its fullest potential.

Below is a brief guide to the steps we just covered in our introduction to Chironic Healing:

Face down:

- ♦ Clear and protect the area in which you are going to work. Ask Source for you to be a channel for healing.

- ♦ Surround yourself and your client in a bubble of light, then a silver bubble.

- ♦ Balance the top diamond and bottom diamond, with emphasis at the top.

- ♦ Stretch the three major lines.

- ♦ Realign and balance the triangles.

- ♦ Balance the sacrum.

Face up:

- ♦ Balance the Mother Points (twenty-six etheric levels).

- ♦ Clear and balance the solar plexus (feeling center).

- ♦ Balance multiple personalities.

- ♦ Balance the TMJ (temporal-mandibular joint).

- ♦ Rebalance top diamond.

Client sitting up:

- ♦ Close off third eye (forehead).

Chironic Healing offers simple and practical steps to many other specific healing processes, both basic and advanced. Areas such as advanced psychic surgery and clearing of past-life trauma are just a couple steps which Chironic Healing makes simple. Most of these advanced techniques are best covered by an experienced teacher. However, in the following paragraphs we'll look at some of them. For further information on books, materials, or lecture schedules by Dr. Trevor Creed, you will find his address and website in Appendix II.

Balancing the Chakras

There are many books and many classes on the practice of balancing the chakras. Chironic Healing makes this process very simple and effective.

With the patient either face up or down, start by surrounding both of your hands in light. Ask Source to assist you in this process. Place one hand over the base chakra, which extends slightly below the tail bone, and place the other hand over the crown chakra above the head. Feel the pulse between the two come into balance. (Refer to Chapter II for a more thorough description of the chakra system.)

At each step, remember to ask Source to balance the chakras. Move on to the second chakra (located just below the navel), and the sixth chakra, just in front or behind the neck area. Repeat the quick balancing procedure. Finally, balance the solar plexus and the heart chakra. Those two are usually the most intense. Allow your hands to be channels of light as you bring them into balance. Balancing the chakras can be that simple.

Now, move on—you have plenty of other work to do.

Psychic Surgery

There have been many claims of healers being able to perform a type of *psychic surgery* on someone with a severe physical ailment. Some have been proven to be fakes or illusionists. The jury is still out on the others.

Chironic Healing approaches psychic surgery from the purely energetic viewpoint, and instead of removing a body part, it chooses to *weave* and heal the underlying energy field. This approach is consistent with all the principles we've laid down in the previous pages.

The steps are basic and simple, but each one must be followed, and done so in order.

1. Muscle test or otherwise determine for certain that Source agrees that you should perform this surgery (weaving).

2. Place a silver essence needle in diamond pt. #1 (see diagram, Figure 6) to anesthetize the patient and hold any pain in check.

3. Bring *purple* energy into the area to slow down the pattern there.

4. Begin to weave the energy just above the area requiring healing. Allow both of your hands to work freely, allowing Source to work through you. Your hands may speed up as they move in gentle circles, weaving and reworking the energy field in this area. Keep going until your hands slow down dramatically—you are finished with this step.

5. With palms down over the area of healing, bring in lots of green energy to heal and balance the work you've just done. Hold this energy for a moment.

6. Finally, placing your hands over the area again, pull them out and up, stretching the energy field and opening it up again. Remember, you slowed it down with purple. Now you must open it again. You are complete.

This technique is especially beneficial for areas of actual surgery, scar tissue, cysts, women who have given birth, have had abortions, etc. It is also excellent for nearly any type of energy blockage that you sense in the area. Simply ask Source for the "okay," and do your magic!

VI

Final
Thoughts

We have focused on the basic principles of healing energy and spiritual law, and have provided the reader with some specific examples and techniques of proven, successful methodologies as well. The techniques, meditations, and principles are never a replacement for common sense, nor do they guarantee instant and miraculous cures. However, cures of this nature are entirely possible and happen frequently. After all, what is seen as a miracle by one may be the natural result of a simple, natural healing technique by another. In other words, a miracle is only relative to the expectation. *A miraculous cure is "miraculous" due to the expectation. These expectations are based on our upbringing, past experience, and current attitudes toward health and healing. Taking this a step further, a high expectation fuels our positive intention, and sets up the required energy and attitude for excellent results.* This effect is true in all of the processes in our lives.

As we begin to understand the underlying principles of health, we begin to see the causative factors behind most diseases, and our treatments will address more quickly the cause rather than the symptom. I have provided a number of examples of this process throughout the text as reference for the reader in this context. Again, some of the key issues are attitude and feeling—these areas of the individual must always be reviewed when addressing and curing an illness, especially one that is of a chronic nature.

All of the principles, *laws*, and techniques we've been discussing throughout the text provide one with the necessary tools to begin to heal—tools that will help you heal others, and heal yourself as well. It is up to you to begin the healing process—to take those first steps, or, for those already on the path, to continue on the path of healing—a path filled with joy, love, and excitement.

Conscious healing does indeed accelerate the healer's growth in many wonderful ways and helps him or her to expand and experience a greater force and a greater depth within. And, after all, that's one of our primary reasons for being here—to experience and to grow! We must always encourage and allow the acts of healing to be joyous and fun.

Our attitude as healers has a far greater effect on the patient than we usually recognize. Often, I am somewhat tired, or perhaps not at my best when asked to perform an energy session on someone. Without fail, not only is the patient rejuvenated, but I am uplifted as well. It is always true that, when we ask Source to be a channel, a conduit for healing, we receive tremendous healing to our being as well. It is one of the great *Laws of Healing*. When we posture ourselves with joy and excitement in the healing environment, we attract the highest vibrations and energies to us to aid us and uplift us in our work.

The Tools for Healing

One of the risks we now face is allowing ourselves to become fragmented or confused over which method or technique to seek out. Almost daily there are new and innovative methods and techniques arriving on the scene. Just in the past few years such methods as magnet therapy, vibrational medicines, holographic imaging, Network Chiropractic, etc., have come on the scene, and this is just the tip of the iceberg. They all seem to have their benefits, and most do not hesitate to let you know that! But it can be overwhelming choosing one if you're feeling bad—this one might work for a friend, this one works for you, this one worked last week, this one was on CNN—you get the point.

One relevant key in all of this is simple: what works for you now? Forget if it works for someone else, and don't worry that it worked for you last year, and no longer works. Your body is changing—but actually more than that, your energy, your vibrations are changing. A technique that worked for you last year may be already *outdated for you now*. That doesn't mean it isn't viable for another, but only that *you've changed*, your energy has changed, and the modality doesn't work any more.

I have seen many people go to a new doctor each week, seeking that one special treatment that cures them, that one special doctor. My answer to that is, yes, by all means seek a doctor or treatment that you like and of which you are sure that there will be results, but if you have a chronic problem, don't expect any treatment or physician to *fix* it overnight. Chronic problems that took years to manifest as symptoms take a reasonable length of time to heal.

As for the various new techniques that have surfaced recently, I believe every modality has some merit. Test each one for yourself. I remain convinced that the underlying causative factors in disease are based in the emotional body (feelings) and the mental body (thoughts). When the feelings and the thoughts are cleansed and realigned, then, coupled with a good modality, long-term healing is the result. As mentioned in the previous pages, there are always a few exceptions to this premise.

The healing experience is a spiritual experience in the truest sense of the word. It can be uplifting beyond all description and evokes the highest, purest elements of our own being. *Love is the basis of all healing,* and in that consciousness, *healing is love in action!*

At the very essence of our being lies a Soul on an infinite journey of discovery and experience. This Soul knows its path, its destiny, and the potential expression in our earthly environment.

You are that Soul incarnate, a manifestation of spiritual essence. When you are in harmony with these elements of your Soul, your life is balanced, content, and all aspects of your expression are healthy. Your Soul is the healer.

Appendix I

Studies

D escribed here are five different experiences I've had with a variety of healing processes. Each is somewhat different, and will demonstrate to the reader the potential for healing in a number of situations. I want to stress that not all sessions are as successful as those below, but I believe that all have the potential for success, depending on all the factors we've been discussing in this book.

Subject A

This middle-aged female approached me and addressed a variety of serious symptoms: frequent asthma attacks, chronic sinus problems, chronic fatigue, chronic poor digestion, high blood toxicity, leaky gut, and more. Because of the multitude of techniques employed and the ongoing work of healing on this patient, I'll touch on just some of the highlights.

In my first session with the woman, I felt much disturbance in the solar plexus area, and throughout all of the digestive tract. Upon questioning her, I discovered that she had had a major intestinal operation in which most most of her digestive tract was actually removed and then reinserted during exploratory surgery. Naturally this operation cause a great disturbance in her system, her life pattern, and in her digestive process. I immediately checked for the affirmative to perform psychic surgery, and was given the green light. (See Chapter V for the psychic surgery protocol.) Subsequent to this session I tested her often, and repeated this procedure three or four times for her abdominal areas. During this first session I also performed much work on her feeling pattern, using much purple essence, and I balanced all the points in her diamond that related to digestion.

Knowing her history with asthma, I also focused on her heart center, lungs, and respiration. I brought into her diamond a cream color, or essence, that helped to balance the toxicity of her system. I added a silver bubble around her entire pattern, and filled it also with this cream essence, using this basic protocol for a few sessions. Her energy level slowly improved, as did her digestion. Her asthma improved more dramatically, but much of the relief for this problem was probably the result of her working in parallel with a naturopathic doctor. I believe the two modalities together provided the boost to her respiratory system.

After six to eight weeks she had improved, but her leaky gut was still draining her energies. As I worked on her solar plexus area, it occurred to me to "seal" her abdomen, and specifically her colon. I visualized the silver essence surrounding her colon so that no energy could leak out. I also sealed her entire abdomen, like a large belt on the outside of her body, to hold her energy in that area. This makes total sense, since each physical part has an etheric counterpart—seal the counterpart, and you seal the physical! I also surrounded her hands and feet with silver and asked Source to seal these extremities for leaky energy as well. This worked quite well, and her energy level reached a new and stable plateau. This new energy level was allowing her body to begin to more quickly heal itself. Her attitude improved greatly, enhancing her whole being.

Other general techniques that worked for her were: visualizing the acupuncture meridians being opened and flowing by running my finger up and down the line (i.e., liver, large intestine, spleen, and stomach), bringing in the essence of yellow in her solar plexus area by swirling my hand, finger downward, over her abdomen and visualizing yellow going in to her solar plexus chakra, and eventually throughout all of her abdominal area. In nearly all of these techniques, this patient could feel the energy moving in the area I was working on. She was extremely sensitive and open to this type of healing. She has improved dramatically since I first met her. She now travels, takes, vacations, and enjoys much more of what life has to offer. My treatments with her were in conjunction with her being treated by a chiropractor, a massage therapist, and a naturopathic doctor.

This patient took some time to heal because all of her symptoms were chronic. It took many years for them to get to the point of being this "layered," and it took quite a few sessions to get to the core of each issue. It was worth it, however.

Subject B

This subject saw me during an introductory workshop in Chironic Healing, and presented quite a blockage in her throat chakra. She was somewhat frail, was a heavy smoker, and didn't express herself very well verbally.

My focus on her was working in her throat chakra; I tested for psychic surgery there and it worked very well. I brought in a lot of white light energy, as well as some blue in that area. When she sat us she said she felt quite well, but there was no obvious change, other than she looked somewhat revitalized. After a lunch break, she returned and told the group that during lunch she had a small coughing attack, and coughed up much mucous. It was obvious that she spoke more clearly— and more importantly, more confidently.

She returned to another workshop about four weeks later. Before I sat her up after a basic session, I asked Source if there was anything left to do. I was drawn again to her throat area, since it felt to still have some blockage there. Inwardly, I saw something quite unique. There appeared to me, in my mind, a type of metal plate through her neck, perpendicular to her body. It was about three-feet square and about one-inch thick. Obviously this was at some type of psychic or etheric level, but it was a clear sign to me that for some reason there was a definite break, a type of disconnect at her throat area.

I muscle tested her to see if it was permissible for me to remove the block. It tested in the affirmative. I intuitively decided to use the silver essence in a type of *ray* method from my fingertip. More specifically, I placed my left palm out and up in a receptive mode, asking to drawn on the patient's own twenty-fifth level. I then pointed my right forefinger toward the plate and visualized the silver essence energy flow from my finger, distinguishing the plate, much like putting out a fire with a water hose. It apparently worked very well. The plate disappeared entirely. At the close of the session, the patient got up and walked to her seat quite easily. The group noticed a remarkable difference in the clarity of her voice, her posture, her skin coloring, and her overall energy level. The block was removed, and her body was "reconnected." She appeared physically to be quite a different person, as she was much clearer and more vibrant. Her voice was clear, and she spoke with great confidence.

When these types of blockages are discovered, I don't try to determine how or why they are there, but only what method is best to deal with the blockage. I don't think we need to know all of the details. I try to focus on the perfect condition, without worrying about all of the issues or situations that created the block initially.

Subject C

This is an example of the power of love, intention, and absent healing. When I was first engaged to be married, my wife's oldest daughter became extremely resistant, and sometimes defiant about my being part of their life—both her life and her mother's life. It was obvious to me and her mother that underneath the outside behaviors were jealousy, fear of abandonment, and a host of other emotional issues.

What came to mind was to use our powers of love and absent healing, and begin to send her light each morning during our morning prayer/meditation session. As that progressed, her poor behavior episodes became less frequent, and many times she actually was very receptive to me. To the light energy we were sending her, I added pink essence, the essence of love. I was thinking that at the core of her being she needed to feel more loved, at least from a male-figure perspective. This indeed seemed to help the healing process. We performed this healing each morning, without fail. No matter what the behaviors were during the day, we never missed a morning of light work with her.

Also, during this time period, I was communicating with her High Self, telling her such things as "I am not taking your mother from you," or "I am not wanting to be your father, just a good friend," etc. We now have a much better relationship, with very few unhealthy incidents. The prayers and meditations along with her mother's verbal discussions brought enormous healing to this child, as well as peace to all of the relationships involved.

Subject D

This is the patient that I referenced in the text who was ready to undergo exploratory surgery for a possible malignant brain tumor. In 1990 I was asked to join two other healers (in two different states) to perform simultaneous absent healing on this patient.

I had not been trained, nor had any experience in Chironic Healing at that time, and was relying greatly on my intuition and my previous experiences in healing. When I sat down on the first occasion and brought the patient's name to my mind, I instantly saw a gray "lump" of something in a certain area of her head. Later, I found that this location was indeed the exact location of the tumor. I intentionally did not put any energy into this vision or lump after I first saw it. I only put light energy and healing into the area.

My first step was to ask Source to be a healing channel for this person; then I saw this person very happy and joyful, full of health and vitality. I next brought in the light energy, followed by a green healing essence. Finally, I invoked what is called the "violet flame." I called to one of the Masters, St. Germain, to assist me in this effort. I visualized a flame of violet essence surrounding and engulfing her entire head area. I asked that all blockages, not of her highest good, be transmuted and eliminated from her energy field.

We performed this healing work on her on two occasions, the second being two days before her preoperation exam. During this exam, her surgeon could not find any trace of her tumor, nor any reason to operate. The three of us were obviously overfilled with joy that we could assist her in the healing process, and we thanked Source for all the support as well!

Subject E

This subject was a lady in her sixties who had many chronic problems, including arthritis, carpal tunnel syndrome, and asthma. She was very positive and bubbly person, but clearly had some emotional issues from her past that lay underneath these outer symptoms.

I worked on nearly all of her issues with a very good measure of success, but will focus on just two here. The first issue was her carpal tunnel syndrome, located in and around her right wrist. She wore an elastic band to support her wrist, and complained of pain with any movement of her right hand.

After the general preliminary work with her lines, diamond, and triangles, I applied some vibrating pressure to her large intestine meridian point, located near the center of the large muscle on the lateral side of her forearm. I then traced all of the meridians in the arm, moving my finger up and down the arm, asking Source to direct the energy of each meridian in the proper direction. I placed silver essence needles in the top diamonds titled "right extremities," and "left extremities." I then placed my right hand over the inflamed area, palm down, and my left hand under the area, palm up. I envisioned a stream of green essence energy flowing from my right hand, through the blocked area, then into my left hand—not unlike a flow of electricity.

As a final step, I used my visualization to place etheric acupuncture needles along her arm leading up to the wrist, and surrounded the area of pain with many other etheric acupuncture needles. This latter placement had no real pattern, other than where I felt they should go.

This was my first treatment on her wrist, and it was very productive. As she walked back into the lobby, she was showing all of the staff there how she could move her wrist quite freely, with absolutely no pain.

The other key area I worked with was her asthma/chest problem. She seemed to breathe very shallow breaths. I had worked in this area twice before, but with no real success. I had worked in the lung point of the diamond, the lung meridian, the heart chakra, etc. She always felt better, but her breathing was still somewhat shallow.

On the third session, I felt a blockage area between her torso and her lower legs, the area near where the large thigh muscles attach to the pelvic bone. I was weaving energy here when suddenly she exclaimed that she could feel a wonderful energy move up through her lungs. She took a deep breath and became ecstatic that she could breathe again! This was the first deep breath she could remember taking since she was a child.

I learned from this session that not only should we never limit or restrain ourselves from working on an area that we feel needs it, but that the energy pattern, as our physical body, is so extremely interrelated with the various parts. I was not working near her lung area, when suddenly the connection between her lower torso and her upper legs opened up, allowing her to breathe deeply and calmly. Months later, when I followed up on her, this stable condition appeared to be permanent.

Appendix II

References for Healers

The Healing Principles of Chiron by Andrew and Trevor Creed
  Chiron Clinic
  Corner, Banyan & Merri Street
  Warrnambool, Victoria 3280, Australia
  www.chironic.com.au

Esoteric Healing by Alice Bailey
  Lucis Publishing Trust
  P.O. Box 722, Cooper Station
  New York, NY 10276

Hands of Light by Barbara Brennan
  Bantam Books
  666 Fifth Avenue
  New York, NY 10103

You Can Heal Your Life by Louise L. Hay
  Hay House
  1242 Berkeley Street
  Santa Monica, CA 90404

Who's the Matter with Me by Alice Steadman
 DeVorss & Company
 P.O. Box 550
 Marina del Rey, CA 90294

The Harmonics of Color, Sound, and Vibration
 by William David
 DeVorss & Company
 P.O. Box 550
 Marina del Rey, CA 90294

Gray's Anatomy
 Crown Publishers, Inc.
 One Park Avenue
 New York, NY 10016

The Spiritual Properties of Herbs by Gurudas
 Cassandra Press
 P.O. Box 868
 San Rafael, CA 94915

Index

Aura Energy for Health, Healing & Balance

Joe H. Slate, Ph.D.

Imagine an advanced energy/information system that contains the chronicle of your life—past, present, and future. By referring to it, you could discover exciting new dimensions to your existence. You could uncover important resources for new insights, growth, and power.

You possess such a system right now. It is your personal aura. In his latest book, Dr. Joe H. Slate illustrates how each one of us has the power to see the aura, interpret it, and fine-tune it to promote mental, physical, and spiritual well-being. College students have used his techniques to raise their grade-point averages, gain admission to graduate programs, and eventually get the jobs they want. Now you can use his aura empowerment program to initiate an exciting new spiral of growth in all areas of your life.

1-56718-637-8
288 pp., 6 x 9
$12.95

Aura Reading for Beginners
Develop Your Psychic Awareness for Health & Success

Richard Webster

When you lose your temper, don't be surprised if a dirty red haze suddenly appears around you. If you do something magnanimous, your aura will expand. Now you can learn to see the energy that emanates off yourself and other people through the proven methods taught by Richard Webster in his psychic training classes.

Learn to feel the aura, see the colors in it, and interpret what those colors mean. Explore the chakra system, and how to restore balance to chakras that are over- or under-stimulated. Then you can begin to imprint your desires into your aura to attract what you want in your life.

These proven methods for seeing the aura will help you: interpret the meanings of colors in the aura, find a career that is best suited for you, relate better to the people you meet and deal with, enjoy excellent health, discover areas of your life that you need to work on, imprint what you want in your future into your aura, make aura portraits with pastels or colored pencils, discover the signs of impending ill health, change the state of your aura and stimulate specific chakras through music, crystals, and color.

1-56718-798-6
208 pp., 5³⁄₁₆ x 8, illus.
$7.95

To Order, Call 1-800-THE MOON
Prices subject to change without notice

Energy Focused Meditation
Body, Mind, Spirit

Genevieve Lewis Paulson
Formerly titled *Meditation and Human Growth*

Meditation has many purposes: healing, past life awareness, balance, mental clarity, and relaxation. It is a way of opening into areas that are beyond your normal thinking patterns. In fact, what we now call "altered states" and "peak experiences"—tremendous experiences of transcendental states—can become normal occurrences when you know how to contact the higher energy vibrations.

Most people think that peak experiences happen, at best, only a few times in life. Through meditation, however, it is possible to develop your higher awareness so you can bring more peak happenings about by concentrated effort. *Energy Focused Meditation* is full of techniques for those who wish to claim those higher vibrations and expanded awareness for their lives today.

1-56718-512-6
224 pp., 6 x 9, 17 illus.
$12.95

To Order, Call 1-800-THE MOON
Prices subject to change without notice

A Chakra & Kundalini Workbook

Psycho-Spiritual Techniques for Health, Rejuvenation, Psychic Powers and Spiritual Realization

Dr. Jonn Mumford
(Swami Anandakapila Saraswati)

Spend just a few minutes each day on the psycho-physiological techniques in this book and you will quickly build a solid experience of inner relaxation that will lead to better health, a longer life, and greater control over your personal destiny. Furthermore, you will lay a firm foundation for the subsequent chapters leading to the attainment of supernormal powers (i.e., photographic memory, self-anesthesia, and mental calculations), an enriched Inner Life, and ultimate transcendence. Learn techniques to use for burnout, mild to moderate depression, insomnia, general anxiety and panic attacks, and reduction of mild to moderate hypertension. Experience sex for consciousness expansion, ESP development, and positive thinking. The text is supplemented with tables and illustrations and a twelve-week practice schedule referenced directly back to the first nine chapters.

A Chakra & Kundalini Workbook is one of the clearest, most approachable books on Yoga there is. Tailored for the Western mind, this is a practical system of personal training for anyone in today's active and complex world.

1-56718-473-1
296 pp., 7 x 10, 8 color plates
$17.95

To Order, Call 1-800-THE MOON

The Energy Body Connection
The Healing Experience of Self-Embodiment

Pamela Welch, M.A.

Illness, unresolved emotional issues, and mental patterns that no longer serve you are actually coded messages from your own soul. *The Energy Body Connection* teaches you the truth about these major soul imprints and shows you how to break the code!

This embodiment process acknowledges emotions and physical problems as signposts of transformation. Instead of denying them, restructure their energy patterns, awakening your body's cells and tissues through the infusion of a spiritual presence.

Powerful exercises in each chapter help you to discover the meaning of your essential soul patterns, experience your chakra energy centers, direct your consciousness to obtain the results you desire, listen to your body's wisdom, access the healing messages contained in your dreams, work with healing light and color, and meet your spirit guides.

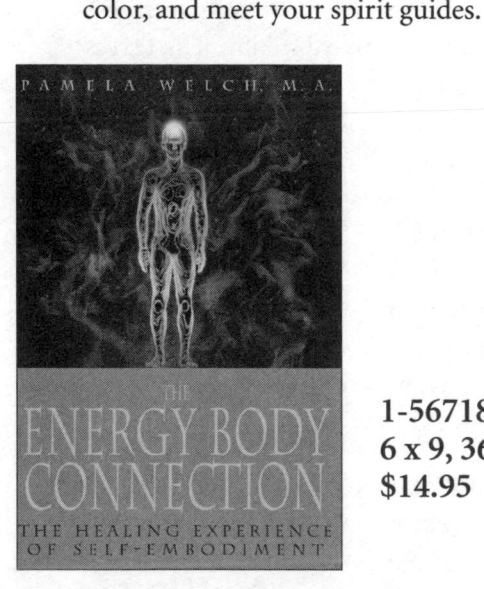

1-56718-819-2
6 x 9, 360 pp.
$14.95

To Order, Call 1-800-THE MOON
Prices subject to change without notice

Reiki for Beginners

Mastering Natural Healing Techniques

David F. Vennels

Reiki is a simple yet profound system of hands-on healing developed in Japan during the 1800s. Millions of people worldwide have already benefited from its peaceful healing intelligence that transcends cultural and religious boundaries. It can have a profound effect on health and well-being by re-balancing, cleansing, and renewing your internal energy system.

Reiki for Beginners gives you the very basic and practical principles of using Reiki as a simple healing technique, as well as its more deeply spiritual aspects as a tool for personal growth and self-awareness. Unravel your inner mysteries, heal your wounds, and discover your potential for great happiness. Follow the history of Reiki, from founder Dr. Mikao Usui's search for a universal healing technique, to the current development of a global Reiki community. Also included are many new ideas, techniques, advice, philosophies, contemplations, and meditations that you can use to deepen and enhance your practice.

1-56718-767-6
264 pp., 5³⁄₁₆ x 8, illus.
$12.95

To Order, Call 1-800-THE MOON

Prices subject to change without notice